T0358255

Cambridge Elements ≡

Elements in Earth System Governance
edited by
Frank Biermann
Utrecht University
Aarti Gupta
Wageningen University

REMAKING POLITICAL INSTITUTIONS: CLIMATE CHANGE AND BEYOND

James J. Patterson
Utrecht University

CAMBRIDGE
UNIVERSITY PRESS

CAMBRIDGE
UNIVERSITY PRESS

University Printing House, Cambridge CB2 8BS, United Kingdom

One Liberty Plaza, 20th Floor, New York, NY 10006, USA

477 Williamstown Road, Port Melbourne, VIC 3207, Australia

314–321, 3rd Floor, Plot 3, Splendor Forum, Jasola District Centre,
New Delhi – 110025, India

79 Anson Road, #06–04/06, Singapore 079906

Cambridge University Press is part of the University of Cambridge.

It furthers the University's mission by disseminating knowledge in the pursuit of
education, learning, and research at the highest international levels of excellence.

www.cambridge.org
Information on this title: www.cambridge.org/9781108708425

First published 2021

A catalogue record for this publication is available from the British Library.

ISBN 978-1-108-70842-5 Paperback
ISSN 2631-7818 (online)
ISSN 2631-780X (print)

Cambridge University Press has no responsibility for the persistence or accuracy of
URLs for external or third-party internet websites referred to in this publication
and does not guarantee that any content on such websites is, or will remain,
accurate or appropriate.

Remaking Political Institutions: Climate Change and Beyond

Elements in Earth System Governance

DOI: 10.1017/9781108769341
First published online: January 2021

James J. Patterson
Utrecht University

Author for correspondence: James J. Patterson, j.j.patterson@uu.nl

Abstract: Institutions are failing in many areas of contemporary politics, not least of which concerns climate change. However, remedying such problems is not straightforward. Pursuing institutional improvement is an intensely political process, which plays out over extended timeframes, and is intricately tied to existing setups. Moreover, such activities are open-ended, and outcomes are often provisional and indeterminate. The question of institutional improvement, therefore, centers on understanding how institutions are *(re)made* within complex and nonideal settings. This Element develops an original analytical foundation for studying institutional remaking and its political dynamics. First, it explains how institutional remaking can be observed. Second, it provides a typology comprising five key areas of institutional production involved in institutional remaking: novelty, uptake, dismantling, stability, and interplay. This opens up a new research agenda on the politics of responding to institutional breakdown, and brings sustainability scholarship into closer dialogue with scholarship on processes of institutional change and development.

This title is also available as Open Access on Cambridge Core

Keywords: institutional change, transformation, institutional development, path dependence, governance

ISBNs: 9781108708425 (PB), 9781108769341 (OC)
ISSNs: 2631-7818 (online), 2631-780X (print)

Contents

1 Introduction   1

2 Institutional Pressure, Institutional Change?   14

3 The Notion of Institutional Remaking   25

4 Observing Institutional Remaking   32

5 Political Dynamics in Institutional Remaking   39

6 Advancing the Study of Institutional Remaking   60

7 Conclusions   69

References   73

1 Introduction

Existing institutions are deeply challenged by many long-standing and emerging changes in contemporary political life. This leads to weaknesses and failures that are being increasingly witnessed across a variety of domains. In particular, climate change stands out as a manifest example, given the urgent need for climate action across the globe. We need to understand how existing institutions can be "remade" in order to address institutional breakdown, particularly in the domestic political sphere. Yet, doing so requires developing a suitable analytical foundation for studying institutional intervention as a political endeavor.

This Element develops an original approach to understanding how political systems can move beyond institutional failure in turbulent but gridlocked contemporary governance contexts. It does so by investigating the political dynamics that occur during attempts to remake political institutions, considering multiple coexisting "areas of institutional production." The notion of *remaking institutions* is proposed as a way of apprehending the intentional and ongoing work involved in contesting, rethinking, and redeploying institutions, and the challenges of doing so within complex existing institutional settings. Thereby, it emphasizes the unfolding and open-ended character of such activities, which are often, as a result, provisional and indeterminate. An exploratory conceptual argument is presented, which probes existing theory and empirical experience (drawing on climate change as an illustrative example), to develop an analytical foundation for studying institutional remaking.

Importantly, the practice of institutional remaking is not in itself a new phenomenon; it is of course the reality of institutional life that intentional changes are almost always pursued within a historical context as well as a larger system of cognate rules. However, what is lacking is appropriate conceptualization of what exactly occurs during such processes, particularly when end states are not necessarily known a priori, or are sharply contested (or both). This issue takes on particular significance in the context of multiplying institutional weaknesses and failures in contemporary society, as well as the (often urgent) imperative for prospective improvement looking forward into the future.

1.1 Institutions in a Changing World

Institutions provide stability for political affairs, but in a rapidly changing world, we increasingly expect institutions to change in order to cope with new pressures, and even anticipate new challenges. Climate change brings this problem into stark relief, as institutions of domestic and global politics are central for not only enabling wise societal decision-making in the face of unprecedented (and even existential) threat, but are also themselves undermined by the changing circumstances brought about by climate change, which are beginning to reverberate throughout human societies. For example, climate impacts threaten not only lives, infrastructure, and ecosystems but also property rights, social stability, and faith in politics. Elsewhere, institutional shortcomings are also at the center of many other major issues facing societies across the globe, such as migration, economic change, digitization, and aging societies. Altogether, these issues expose weaknesses and failures in contemporary political systems that seem increasingly incapable, and often were simply not built for, the new and emerging pressures they now face. Yet, understanding how political institutions can be reformed, renewed, and reinvented – in other words, "remade" – is a major challenge.

1.2 The Case of Climate Change

In the case of climate change, political institutions are central to addressing and responding to the profound risks posed. Scientists and policymakers argue evermore strongly that societies must embark on major reorganizations – commonly described as "societal transformations" – in order to mitigate and adapt to climate change (IPCC, 2018; NCE, 2018; Patterson et al., 2017; Pelling, 2011; Scoones et al., 2015). This is especially vital for constraining temperature rises to globally agreed targets of 1.5–2°C, beyond which unstoppable or runaway climate impacts are likely to be triggered.[1] It requires "decarbonizing" systems of production and consumption across all sectors and levels of human activity, and adapting social, political, and economic systems to fundamentally shifting boundary conditions in a climate-changed world. Such transformations may relate to a particular goal (e.g., decarbonization, adaptation), policy sector (e.g., energy, mobility, water, food, built environment), or aspect of society (e.g., technology, economy, culture). As climate change impacts grow in magnitude and severity across the globe, these impacts themselves are likely to become a structural *cause* of transformation in human societies, at the same time as being *driven* by human societies. This leads to a curious situation where societal transformation is now bound to occur one way or another: Either transformation

---

[1] A limit of +2°C average global warming has long been used as a shorthand for avoiding unstoppable climate feedback and tipping points (such as the melting of ice sheets and Arctic permafrost), which are impossible to reverse. A limit of +1.5°C, as recognized in the 2015 global Paris Agreement, is believed to be required to protect low-lying island states from being submerged and their peoples permanently displaced, and to provide a higher margin for avoiding critical thresholds and tipping points (Conference of the Parties, 2015). Although, both limits are probabilistic, so the avoidance of tipping points is still not guaranteed.

is pursued intentionally in order to limit and curtail climate change or transformation is forced on societies as a result of failing to limit climate change with profound disruption triggered as a result (Fazey et al., 2018).

However, while intentional transformations are urgently called for,[2] understanding *how* they may come about – beginning from the imperfect conditions of the present and in the face of often intense contestation – is deeply challenging. Among scholars, the focus so far has mostly been either, on the one hand, describing problems and the need for transformation or, on the other hand, advocating normative visions for a sustainable future. However, the *processes of change* by which such transformations could actually be realized remain vastly under-theorized, a gap that is especially significant for institutions given their central role in structuring political decision-making.

The problem structure of climate change creates a vexing political challenge. The diffuse nature of climate change impacts across societies and over time, as well as the dilemma that rapid and ambitious climate action requires societies to accept concentrated costs now in exchange for avoiding uncertain and dispersed costs in the future, has proven to be a critical barrier to domestic climate change action over decades (Jacobs, 2016; Stokes, 2016; Victor, 2011). Crucially, this is not just a question of aggregate interests, preferences, and social choice. It is also rooted more fundamentally in the political institutions that structure and channel political decision-making. Political institutions that are implicated include not only those specifically concerned with climate change governance but also broader political institutions that influence social choices about climate change. The resulting sets of incentives/sanctions, norms/goals, and practices/behaviors cultivated by political institutions shape the ways in which societies make decisions and conduct climate action.

Realizing societal transformations under climate change, therefore, involves changes in political institutions in response to, as well as in anticipation of, climate change destabilization. For example, Hausknost and Hammond (2020, p. 4) argue that "a rapid, purposeful, and comprehensive decarbonization of modern society without the force of law and without adequate institutions of deliberation, will-formation, decision-making, policy coordination, and enforcement seems highly unlikely." Changes in political institutions are needed in three key areas:

1. Political institutions in a given society need to *adapt* to changing circumstances, including material-environmental boundary conditions and their related social, economic, and geopolitical impacts.

---

[2] The Intergovernmental Panel on Climate Change (IPCC) recently concluded that drastic action was required within just 12 years to have even a 66 percent chance of meeting the 1.5–2°C global target (IPCC, 2018).

2. "Specific" political institutions of climate change governance (e.g., policies, programs, law/regulation) need to support *anticipatory* climate action that is rapid and ambitious.
3. "General" political institutions (e.g., policy-making processes, legislatures, systems of representation and deliberation, authorities, constitutions) need to support *long-term decision-making* capable of addressing systemic challenges and avoiding short-termism.

The first point concerns primarily *reactive* changes to develop institutions that are fit for purpose within profoundly changing circumstances. The second and third points concern *anticipatory* changes to develop institutions that are fit for navigating the future. The key question, of course, is how such changes can be realized.

1.3 "Remaking" Institutions

The need to remake institutions in a rapidly changing world is a core challenge for contemporary governance. For example, Busby (2018) observes that "the world seems to be in state of permanent crisis," which brings issues of institutional weakness and failure to the forefront of debates about how societies may cope with ongoing disruption. Yet, while institutional shortcomings are increasingly identified, scholars and policymakers alike seem equally puzzled about how solutions may be found and realized.

Climate change impacts are already occurring with increasing intensity and frequency,[3] including extreme floods, droughts and hurricanes, more severe and widespread wildfires, and rapidly melting glaciers in mountain regions across the globe. Yet climate change governance, both domestically and globally, remains sluggish. Second-order pressures on institutions are also likely due to destabilization of societal and political systems, such as in regard to loss of property rights (Freudenberger and Miller, 2010; McGuire, 2019), impacts on health (Sellers et al., 2019; Whitmee et al., 2015), disrupted global supply chains (Ghadge et al., 2020), forced migration (Berchin et al., 2017), contribution to intra- or inter-state conflict (Devlin and Hendrix, 2014; Gleick, 2014; Nardulli et al., 2015), impacts on access to food (Ericksen et al., 2009), new geopolitical tensions (Busby, 2018; Hommel and Murphy, 2013), and even an erosion of trust by citizens in democratic political systems themselves due to the

---

[3] While attribution of singular events to climate change is an ongoing and challenging area of scientific research, cumulative patterns of destructive climatic events already witnessed are increasingly attributed to climate change, and are also exemplary of what is expected under climate change; indeed, these patterns frequently exceed scientific expectations in pace and severity.

failure of governments to tackle climate change over many years (Brown et al., 2019).

Institutional challenges also abound beyond climate change. For example, irregular migration has tested global systems of migration and human rights protections in recent years, as global conflicts and/or repressive regimes have triggered waves of refugee movements, with sometimes volatile political reactions such as rising populist sentiments. In Europe, for example, current arrangements allocating responsibility for sharing refugee arrivals are tenuous, and further stresses (including as a result of climate impacts) could be untenable (Werz and Hoffman, 2016). More broadly, economic insecurity of citizens is a growing source of anxiety in many countries, linked to both domestic economic policies and global economic changes, such as economic restructuring over decades under globalization (e.g., offshoring of jobs, deindustrialization, automation), raising questions about the durability of labor and social welfare institutions (Bregman, 2018; Wright, 2010). Additionally, aging societies create large slow-moving future challenges with growing mismatches between state pension liabilities and the productive base of workers needed to sustain them, especially in many industrialized countries, which has implications for social security and healthcare institutions (Bloom, 2019; de Mooij, 2006). Together, this indicates a critical need to understand how institutions in many areas of political affairs can be intentionally remade over the coming years and decades.

Yet, while institutional solutions are needed for many problems, exactly how such solutions can be realized in practice – even when prescribed – is not well understood. Most broadly, institutions refer to "the rules of the game in a - society"[4] (North, 2010, p. 3), "established and prevalent social rules that structure social interactions" (Hodgson, 2006, p. 2), or "persistent rules that shape, limit, and channel human behavior" (Fukuyama, 2014, p. 6). More specifically, institutions are defined as "clusters of rights, rules and decision-making procedures that give rise to social practices, assign roles to the participants in these practices, and guide interactions among occupants of these roles" (Young et al., 2008, p. xxii). In other words, institutions refer to the rules mediating interactions among actors in a given decision-making arena,[5] including both formal and informal aspects (Ostrom, 2005). Importantly, such rules are not solely instrumental but are also "embedded in structures of meaning"

---

[4] North also makes a helpful distinction between institutions and organizations to avoid their conflation: "Institutions are the rules of the game, organizations are the players" (North, 2010, p. 59).

[5] Following Ostrom (2005), such an arena ("action arena") occurs whenever multiple actors engage in action concerning an issue of joint interest and/or impact, insofar as their individual actions have interdependent consequences. This places analytical focus on empirical situations as they appear, rather than based on a predefined jurisdictional site or scale.

(March and Olsen, 2008, p. 3) and communication (Beunen and Patterson, 2019; Schmidt, 2008). Hence, cultures, routines, and habits also matter (Hodgson, 2006; March and Olsen, 1983). The overall effect of political institutions is to channel individual and collective agency of social actors, and structure procedures of political decision-making. However, institutions are typically understood to be complex, persistent, and difficult to intentionally change. Indeed, by definition, institutions provide stability and emerge from past circumstances, which make them inherently conservative.

What does this mean for remaking institutions to address climate change and other twenty-first-century governance problems? First, it is important to note that intentional action to remake institutions may be pursued at different levels of institutional order.[6] This can include a programmatic level (e.g., policies, plans, agreements), a legislative level (e.g., laws, regulations), and a "constitutional" level (e.g., formal constitutions, courts, electoral and representative systems, fundamental political norms) (following Ostrom, 2005; Rhodes et al., 2008). Action at each respective level may be more or less readily achievable: Programmatic actions are typically easier to realize than legislative action, whereas constitutional action is typically difficult and rare. Changes at each level may also proceed over differing timescales (e.g., years, decades, several decades). Second, attempts to realize intentional institutional change are not only instrumental but also normative and communicative. For example, political justifications, argumentation and legitimation (Beetham, 2013), and buy-in between rule takers and rule enforcers are vital for securing durable changes. Third, institutions are connected to other aspects of society, such as behaviors and practices of social actors, and materiality of technologies and infrastructures (Seto et al., 2016). For example, Bernstein and Hoffman (2018a, p. 248) point out that decarbonization (i.e., the removal of fossil fuels from all systems within society) confronts the problem of "carbon lock-in," which "arises from overlapping technical, political, social, and economic dynamics that generate continuing and taken-for-granted use of fossil energy." Hence, attempts to intentionally change institutions, even when geared toward solving pressing societal problems such as climate change, inevitably involve political contestation and struggle in hetero-geneous societies where different social actors hold varying preferences, inter-ests, values, and worldviews. Consequently, for socio-technical shifts such as decarbonization, the ways in which new systems come to be adopted depends on "how they are assembled and congealed through particular arrangements" (Stripple and Bulkeley, 2019, p. 54), in other words, institutions.

---

[6] Where "order" is understood not as "orderliness" but as "the recognition of patterned regularity in social and political life" (Lieberman, 2002, p. 697).

1.4 Domestic Political Sphere

The domestic political sphere (encompassing national, subnational, and local climate action) is crucial to realizing societal transformations to meet global climate targets. Current global climate policy relies on nations delivering on their commitments made under the 2015 Paris Agreement. Under this agreement, nations are expected to set commitments and undergo reviews on a cyclical basis, to support progressive ratcheting up of ambitions over time, while allowing scrutiny from other nations and civil society along the way (Falkner, 2016). Consequently, the success of global climate action now depends on robust action in the domestic political sphere to translate global commitments, navigate complex societal changes, and advance ambitious climate action.[7] At the same time, the domestic sphere is where climate policies are most directly enacted but also challenged. For example, climate policies may be accepted by societies, but they also may face intense resistance or even backlash (e.g., undermining or repealing of policy, institutional dismantling, social protests, and resistance). Importantly, the domestic (sovereign) sphere is where the authority and capability for remaking many political institutions are ultimately grounded.

Institutional remaking already occurs, or is at least debated, in a variety of ways in domestic politics. Examples include the creation of comprehensive policy frameworks (e.g., measures to structurally support the uptake of renewable energy) (Buchan, 2012), regulation to steer public and private choices (e.g., planning and zoning, building standards, vehicle emissions standards) (Sachs, 2012), sectoral and society-wide legislation (e.g., climate change acts, legislated targets for decarbonization, ratification of national emissions reduction commitments) (Lorenzoni and Benson, 2014), creation of new authorities (e.g., agencies/departments, coordination bodies, independent advisory agencies) (Lorenzoni and Benson, 2014; Patterson et al., 2019), economic restructuring (e.g., active investment policies, removal of fossil fuel subsidies)[8] (Brown and Granoff, 2018), experimentation with new forms of decision-making (e.g., deliberative forums) (Dryzek et al., 2019), and the emergence of climate litigation and its institutional consequences (Peel and Osofsky, 2018; Sharp, 2019). These changes span the three imperatives for remaking institutions under climate that were identified in Section 1.1 (i.e., adapting to changing structural conditions, supporting ambitious climate action, and encouraging comprehensive and long-term political decision-making).

---

[7] Young (2013, p. 97) contends that the success of international regimes "depends on both the capacity and the willingness of members states to implement their requirements in domestic political arenas."

[8] This also relates directly to new policy proposals and debates over a green (new) deal in Europe (European Commission, 2019) and the United States (e.g., Ocasio-Cortez, 2019).

More broadly, intentional efforts to "remake institutions" can also be seen in other domains of political life, both past and present. For example, economic liberalization has been pursued through domestic and global policies over several decades, and domestic spheres have in turn been reshaped by the resulting forces of globalization. Labor, social welfare, agriculture and tax policies have been other major areas of reform and restructuring over recent decades. Democratization has also occurred in a variety of countries (e.g., post-soviet, post-dictatorship, post-conflict). All these changes involve intentional activities to remake political institutions. So far, profound reforms have largely not been emulated for climate change, where institutional remaking has remained relatively nascent. Yet climate change differs from previous analogues because it, at least so far, lacks a singular normative objective which a durable majority of social actors buy into (e.g., as for democratization or liberalization), and it is also highly open-ended without a clear end point for reforms. Lessons from the study of policy reform are also instructive. In examining the post-adoption politics of policy reforms, Patashnik (2014) argues that "the passage of a reform does not settle *anything*" and the "sustainability of reforms turns on the *reconfiguration* of political dynamics" (p. 3, emphases in original). Hence, contestation is central to both introducing but also embedding institutional changes over time. This brings attention to the provisional and indeterminate character of institutional change, and the ongoing political struggles that it entails.

1.5 Focus of This Element

This Element investigates the political dynamics that occur during attempts to remake political institutions, through considering multiple coexisting "areas of institutional production." This begins with viewing institutional intervention as an ongoing political activity, rather than a once-off intervention moment (especially under climate change), which has several implications. First, political institutions act as distributional instruments which generate sites of contestation, leading to a focus on "rule-making" rather than only "rule-taking."[9] Second, institutional remaking is an unfolding process, which may often lack a clear start and end point (e.g., end states are not necessarily known a priori), which implies a need for studying unfolding processes rather than snapshots. Third, given its provisional and indeterminate nature, evaluation of the "success" of institutional remaking at any given moment must recognize partial and incomplete outcomes.

---

[9] Rule-making emphasizes the politics of rule-creation and embedding, whereas rule-taking treats rules as given and examines the behavior of social actors within a given rule set. Thus, a focus on rule-making foregrounds the political nature of institutional intervention, and the struggles over how rules are created and changed in society.

Most broadly, this Element contributes to understanding how societies pursue and realize societal transformations through choice rather than collapse. In other words, how can solutions to institutional problems be found proactively without waiting for catastrophic failure? The problem of climate change is unprecedented in this regard.[10] It demands that societies act in anticipatory ways to take account of systemic, irreversible, and largely future impacts, which extend far beyond any single existing polity. As prominent institutional scholars March and Olsen (2008, p. 12) observe: "In spite of accounts of the role of heroic founders and constitutional moments, modern democracies also seem to have limited capacity for institutional design and reform and in particular for achieving intended effects of reorganizations." Consequently, "we know a lot about polities but not how to fix them" (North, 2010, p. 67). Yet the importance and urgency of addressing climate change can hardly be overstated. Decisions made now are immensely consequential for the future, in a way that overwhelms existing political institutions and defies easy analogy. The challenge of remaking political institutions is both instrumentally and normatively significant. The overall motivation and theoretical terrain for studying institutional remaking, with a focus here on climate change, are shown in Figure 1.

Theoretically, we have rich repertoire of institutional theory to draw on, including a growing range of approaches for explaining institutional change. Nevertheless, our understanding of how institutions can be intentionally remade remains opaque. Institutional theory is typically backward looking as it focuses on explaining past changes (e.g., comparative historical analysis). There is often also a mismatch between narrow empirical explanations (e.g., focusing on single rules) and the reality of institutional multiplicity within real-world decision-making arenas (i.e., complex clusters of rules). Scholars now need to

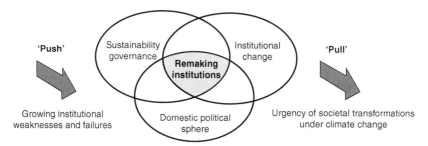

Figure 1 Situating the theoretical challenge of remaking institutions under climate change

---

[10] For example, Newell (2015, p. 72) points out in regard to green transformations: "One obvious challenge to drawing . . . parallels [to previous large-scale transformations in human society such as industrial transformations] lies in the basic fact that no large scale transformation . . . to date has been motivated explicitly by the imperatives of dealing with environmental crises per se."

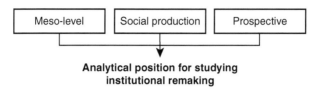

Figure 2 Analytical positioning of the approach to studying institutional remaking

engage with theorizing how institutional solutions are, or could be, enacted within complex and nonideal real-world settings.

To this end, the departure point for the approach developed here combines: (i) a *meso-level* scalar focus, (ii) a *social production* ontology, and (iii) a *prospective* temporal orientation (Figure 2).

First, a meso-level scalar focus refers to concern for *rule clusters* structuring collective decision-making arenas, over timeframes of several years to a decade. It contrasts against a micro-level perspective focusing on the dynamics of individual social actors operating on a day-to-day timeframe and a macro-level perspective focusing on large institutional changes over decadal timeframes; yet it nonetheless recognizes the influence of both micro- and macro-level forces. Micro-level forces (such as change agents) and macro-level forces (such as overarching political structures and paradigms) may both influence meso-level institutional remaking. A meso-level perspective also focuses on institutions and their interactions with human-technological-ecological systems within a polity that has the ability to reshape these institutions to some meaningful extent. For example, such a polity may be delineated at the level of a city, state/province, or a nation. Overall, this challenges us to focus on change in aggregate rule clusters linked to a particular issue.

Second, a social production ontology focuses on the activities through which social action[11] is generated in attempts to address a specific problem. In other words, it locates the analytical challenge at hand as one of understanding how, why, and under which conditions institutional remaking occurs. The notion of social production has been described in urban governance literature as "the power to accomplish tasks" (Mossberger and Stoker, 2001, p. 829), where "the power struggle concerns, not control and resistance, but gaining and fusing a capacity to act – power to, not power over" (Stone, 1989, cited in Stoker and Mossberger 1994, p. 197). Hence this perspective reflects a conception of power as generative. Partzsch (2017) identifies three ideal-type conceptions of power in sustainability

---

[11] This emphasizes that more than one actor is involved, and action therefore involves social interactions, situated within an institutional arena.

transformations: "power with" (cooperation, learning, coaction), "power over" (coercion, manipulation, domination), and "power to" (resistance, empowerment, potential for action by certain agents). A social production perspective mainly aligns with a conception of "power to," as it aims to understand processes of action and change (including resistance).

Third, a prospective temporal orientation refers to a focus on unfolding changes (i.e., both those that are "in-the-making" and those that "could be") and how their future form is shaped by actions in the present. This includes understanding contemporary and past dynamics, which set certain trajectories of change in motion and/or constrain the potential for future changes. Such a perspective challenges institutional scholars to think about how it may be possible to prospectively address complex societal problems. This is vital for understanding how social and political changes, and ultimately transformations, might come about in practice. Crucially, this is not about advocacy, but about analytically understanding how a particular institutional change deemed desirable by certain social actors might be realized. If elucidating the nature and effects of institutions is a "first order" problem and explaining institutional change is a "second order" problem (following Hall, 2010), then understanding *prospective* institutional improvement might usefully be seen as a "third order" problem for institutional scholarship.

From this tripartite starting point, this Element develops an original approach to understanding how political systems can move beyond institutional failure in turbulent but gridlocked contemporary governance contexts. It develops an analytical foundation for studying institutional remaking and its political dynamics, including (i) an evaluation frame to observe institutional remaking and (ii) a heuristic typology comprising multiple key areas of institutional production expected to occur within processes of institutional remaking (i.e., novelty, uptake, dismantling, stability, and interplay). The approach draws on scholarship from political science, environmental studies, and sociology, and fields of research spanning institutional analysis, environmental governance, and sustainability transformations. Altogether, this opens up a new research agenda on the politics of responding to institutional breakdown, to support scholars in finding institutional solutions to contemporary governance problems. It also brings sustainability scholarship into closer dialogue with broader lines of thinking about processes of institutional change and development.

1.6 Overall Argument

The overall argument of this Element is that we need to better understand the processes by which political institutions are remade vis-à-vis weaknesses and failures in order to address many urgent challenges such as climate change.

A key challenge is to probe prospective institutional development in order to not only explain (past) political change, but also to contribute to finding constructive (future) solutions to real-world problems. Political science typically focuses on explaining changes which have already occurred, rather than considering how future changes (and especially improvements, however conceived) might, or could, come about.[12] To engage with future developments often invokes ideas about design, foresight, and anticipation which – while practically useful and theoretically rich – tend to view the future through a metaphor of pathways to be pursued or avoided, arguably implying undue consensus and knowability. An alternative approach, as developed here, is to focus on the *production of social action* in the present, situated within a broader historical trajectory of past experience and future possibility, anchored in unfolding activities that shape the form and directionality of future outcomes.

This locates the problem of institutional remaking as one of understanding how intentional intervention is generated through interactions among a multiplicity of actors within complex institutional arenas. Institutional remaking involves political jockeying and struggle and is entangled with heterogeneous societies, material infrastructures, and changing environmental conditions. Studying it involves grappling with unfolding processes and partial outcomes; accepting that it is, in the fullest sense,[13] ongoing and in-the-making rather than a discrete event. This may be uncomfortable analytical territory for scholars seeking bounded, testable short-term relations. However, there is no inherent reason why institutional remaking cannot be studied from a variety of methodological standpoints, leaning toward theory-testing or theory-building, qualitative/interpretive or quantitative/objective analysis, and exploratory or explanatory reasoning. But to begin with, we must first develop a robust analytical foundation, which is the task of this Element.

The structure of the argument is as follows. Section 1 introduces the notion of institutional remaking and the need for it, both in regard to climate change and more broadly, and outlines key starting points for the argument. Section 2 elucidates pressures on institutions along with barriers to change and synthesizes current thinking about how and why institutional change occurs, which highlights the need for a focus on institutional remaking. Section 3 defines and delineates institutional remaking, situating it as a processual phenomenon, and

---

[12] This critique resonates with a similar plea made to the field of international relations by Busby (2019) concerning the need to study climate change as a "present and prospective" challenge, contrasted against the typical emphasis on "understanding past patterns and drawing inferences."

[13] Essentially, climate change can be seen as imposing a new structural condition for human society across material, political, and even existential dimensions, involving continuous change into the future. In this holistic sense, it resonates closely with the notion of the Anthropocene (e.g., see Dryzek, 2016).

reflecting on the role of intentionality and how this differs compared to institutional design. Section 4 develops a comprehensive frame for observing and evaluating institutional remaking. Section 5 develops a heuristic typology comprising five key areas of institutional production that are expected to play out during processes of institutional remaking, drawing on both sustainability governance and institutional theory. Section 6 identifies insights about processes of intentional institutional change, contributions to broader institutional theory, and research priorities. Section 7 concludes with distilling the overall contributions of the argument.

2 Institutional Pressure, Institutional Change?

Contemporary political institutions experience growing pressures, and yet they do not automatically adjust to cope with these pressures. A variety of barriers to institutional change occur. In response, the topic of institutional change has been an area of major interest among scholars in recent years, with a variety of insights put forward by different communities. However, this is not fully sufficient to understand how institutions can be (intentionally) remade.

2.1 Pressures on Contemporary Institutions

The problem of institutional weakness and/or failure, on climate change as well as a range of other issues, is a core motivation for studying institutional remaking. Here, institutional weakness and/or failure refers to the inadequate performance of actually existing institutions for addressing a certain issue confronting society. For example, in environmental governance, Newig et al. (2019) identify empirical examples of institutional failure including institutional deficiencies contributing to environmental pollution incidents, costly performance of endangered species legislation, and inadequacy for decarbonizing electricity production. In the context of political decentralization reform, Koelble and Siddle (2014) identify examples of institutional failure such as lacking municipal service delivery and democratic deficit due to mismatched municipal capacity. More broadly, Peters (2015) identifies governance failures characterized by poor cooperation either among political elites or between bureaucracies, particularly in the face of issues that are sectorally crosscutting, long term, and/or containing entrenched ideological aspects, which result in "either limited governance outputs, or outputs that are incapable of addressing more than a portion of the problem confronting the public sector and the society" (pp. 263–264). Prakash and Potoski (2016, pp. 118–120) classify several types of institutional failure: failures of design (where the initial setup is unsuitable to regulate the problem), mismatch and obsolescence (where new or altered actors evade existing regulation), failure to adapt (where institutions remain too static over time), and capture (where certain actors gain undue influence over regulation).

Yet a variety of contemporary pressures on political institutions suggest that these risks are unlikely to dissipate anytime soon and in fact are only likely to grow. Such pressures include political stagnation, shifting environmental boundary conditions, and burgeoning societal heterogeneity.

First, scholars highlight worrying patterns of political stagnation in recent years. This is described in a variety of ways, including as gridlock and political decay. For example, at a global level, scholars observe gridlock on a variety of transborder problems (e.g., climate change, trade, finance) hindering global problem-solving (Hale et al., 2013). At a domestic level, the historical development of core political institutions now points toward decay in some countries such as the United States linked to fragmentation, polarization, and abundant opportunities for veto, calling into question the ability of such systems to function effectively (Fukuyama, 2014). Furthermore, rising populism in many countries in recent years (e.g., Norris and Inglehart, 2019; Schaller and Carius, 2019) has implications for climate change. For example, critiques of cosmopolitanism may make it harder to generate public support for ambitious climate action since benefits are questioned, and due to a lack of trust that other countries are also taking commensurate action, even despite the presence of the Paris Agreement as a global coordination arrangement. On the other hand, lack of climate action could erode trust in democratic political systems over time, due to failure of governments to meaningfully address climate change (Brown et al., 2019).

Second, the impacts of climate change are many and varied across global and local geographies, including exposure to climate disasters (e.g., droughts, floods, wildfires, heatwaves) and long-term climate shifts (e.g., changing patterns of rainfall, sea level, and temperatures), and their interaction with human systems (e.g., cities, agriculture, infrastructures). These changes are ongoing and nonlinear. Seemingly small changes may produce large effects (e.g., small changes in atmospheric moisture may have major impacts on the likelihood of floods or droughts). Altogether, this results in shifting environmental boundary conditions for human societies, a problem that has been labelled "nonstationarity." Nonstationarity refers to underlying shifts in long-term climate patterns (i.e., mean, variance), which implies that expected conditions upon which political institutions have developed over decades, and even centuries, no longer apply (Craig, 2010; Milly et al., 2008). Political institutions linked to the production and distribution of resources and even basic rights are threatened. For example, property rights may become devalued or untenable (e.g., water, land, infrastructures) (Freudenberger and Miller, 2010; McGuire, 2019). Implications for political stability are unknown and undoubtably troubling.

Third, societal heterogeneity in contemporary human societies (e.g., in terms of interests, preferences, beliefs, values) deeply challenges the ability of political systems to respond to complex problems such as climate change. Diverging political demands and reactions to policy proposals, and fragmented and polarized public opinion make far-sighted political renewal seem almost like an anachronism in contemporary politics. At the same time, governance itself becomes increasingly multiple. For example, there are now a wide range of non-state and subnational actors involved in climate change governance across domestic, transnational, and global spheres (Abbott, 2012; Bulkeley et al., 2014; Chan et al., 2015; Hale, 2016). Some lines of thinking emphasize difficulties of fragmentation that can result (Biermann et al., 2009; Zelli and van Asselt, 2013). On the other hand, scholars within a pluralist tradition view heterogeneity as a social fact (Aligica, 2014). In this line, the notion of poly-centricity has been taken up recently to try to make sense of dispersed centers of authority in climate change governance (Jordan et al., 2018). Such a view would suggest that institutions are potentially remade in diverse and interdependent ways within complex institutional arenas. Yet it also raises questions about the performance of institutions "in an increasingly interdependent world of diverse and conflicting views, beliefs, preferences, values, and objectives" (Aligica, 2014, p. xiv).

2.2 Barriers to Institutional Change

Despite the pressures identified in Section 2.1, institutions are unlikely to adjust automatically to new circumstances and objectives. Institutions are embedded in historical, political, cultural, and material/environmental set-tings. The weight of the past constrains change because patterns of coordin-ation in political systems tend to persist over time. Institutional change is also typically contested and may be driven by endogenous actors (Mahoney and Thelen, 2010), rapid and slow-moving external forces (Pierson, 2004), and friction with neighboring institutional orders (Orren and Skowronek, 1996). As a result, a variety of barriers to institutional change arise, including path dependency, inefficiency, materiality, and opportunity structures (Table 1). Sustainability scholars typically emphasize path dependency and materiality,

Table 1 Barriers to institutional change

Barrier	Description	Implications
Path dependency	Commitments and incentives lead actors to maintain status quo	Institutions develop mechanisms that reinforce their own stability
Inefficiency	Weak mechanisms of competition, learning, and adaptation	Institutions are inefficient at adjusting to changing circumstances and objectives
Materiality	"Lock-in" of institutions due to socio-material linkages	Institutions are interconnected with environments, infrastructures, and practices
Opportunity structures	Heterogeneous and ephemeral opportunity structures	Institutions are not equally open to change in all areas or moments in time

while institutional scholars typically emphasize path dependency, inefficiency, and opportunity structures. Climate change brings all four into focus.

Perhaps the most commonly cited reason for a lack of institutional adjustment is that of path dependency. This explains how existing institutions contribute to creating incentive and payoff structures that tend to reinforce and perpetuate their own existence; societal actors reconfigure their expectations and capabilities and become invested due to accumulating benefits over time (Pierson, 2004). This creates a dynamic of "increasing returns" where benefits accumulate to actors who are already set up to take advantage of existing arrangements, the costs of switching paths are relatively high, and, therefore, early departure points have persistent consequences down the line (Pierson, 2000a). The reasons why this is difficult to overcome include coordination challenges for those defecting from the existing setup, veto points available at a more fundamental level than the particular arena in question, and commitments built up over time in relation to the current setup such as "relationships, expectations, privileges, knowledge of procedures" (Pierson, 2004, pp. 142–148). Yet, at the same time, the inherent "stickiness" conferred by institutions is helpful to social actors because it allows to "reduce uncertainty and enhance stability, facilitating forms of cooperation and exchange that would otherwise be impossible" (Pierson, 2004, p. 43). Thus, path dependency "is not a story of inevitability in which the past neatly predicts the future" (Pierson, 2004, p. 52) and "is not 'inertia', rather it is the constraints on the choice set in the present that are derived from historical experiences of the past" (North, 2010, p. 52). But altogether, it leads to strong commitments and incentives, especially among incumbent actors, to maintain the status quo.

In the face of path dependency, sustainability scholars often point to the potential for institutional change through mechanisms of competition, learning, and adaptation. However, these mechanisms have all been critiqued as weak in practice for various reasons. Competition is typically assumed to occur within and between decision-making arenas (e.g., cities, nations) over approaches to responding to climate change, a view that is rooted in an evolutionary economics frame. However, political institutions are rarely subject to competition in a classical sense since they "often have a monopoly over a particular part of the political terrain" (Pierson, 2000b, p. 488). Learning is typically assumed to occur within and between decision-making arenas through direct experience (e.g., climate change impacts, changes understood to be needed) or indirect experiences (e.g., observing other decision-making arenas), a view rooted in a sociological frame of interactive social action. However, the relation between new ideas (stemming from learning) and institutional change is not direct (Hall,

1993), and therefore learning is not synonymous with actual changes in governance but should be seen as a separate step (Pierson, 2000b, p. 490). Adaptation is typically assumed to occur when faced with changing circumstances (e.g., experienced or expected climate change impacts), a view rooted partly in a frame of rational response to problems, but also partly in a complexity frame that emphasizes the need for continuous adaptability within dynamic circumstances. However, there is no guarantee that actors will want to adjust to changing circumstances, especially when uncertainties or ambiguities afford cover for retaining existing political positions. Moreover, "because political reality is so complex and the tasks of evaluating public performance and determining which options would be superior are so formidable, such self-correction is often limited" (Pierson, 2000b, p. 490). Altogether, these inefficiencies mean that institutions do not automatically adjust to changing circumstances or societal objectives.

Sustainability scholars emphasize how institutions are closely bound up in assemblages comprising environments, infrastructure/technology, and practices/behaviors. For example, Young (2010a) examines the dynamics of international environmental regimes from the perspective of interactions between endogenous factors and exogenous biophysical and socioeconomic factors, emphasizing their combined role in explaining regime performance. Ostrom (2005, 1990) famously developed a view of institutions as inherently bound up with environmental and social conditions, making clear the need to analyze these dimensions as a package. Elsewhere, the field of sustainability transitions is premised on inseparable links between people, infrastructures, and institutions. For example, Andrews-Speed (2016, p. 217) suggests that "the energy sector can be envisaged as a particular type of socio-technical regime comprising an assemblage of institutions which develop around a particular set of technologies and support the development and use of those technologies," and Stripple and Bulkeley (2019, p. 52) argue that "decarbonisation politics are socio-materially constituted." Indeed, this is an area in which sustainability scholarship enriches broader institutional theory, which often tends to underplay the causal connections between institutions and their material/environmental context by focusing primarily on political and historical explanatory factors. Crucially, what this means is that institutions can be subject to "lock-in," not only for endogenous reasons (such as path dependency and inefficient adjustment), but also because of relations with broader environmental-social-material factors (Monstadt and Wolff, 2015; Seto et al., 2016; Unruh, 2000).

Opportunities for institutional change are typically heterogeneous and ephemeral because of changes in the exogenous context, differences across levels of institutional order, and endogenous dynamism within institutions themselves. Abrupt changes in the exogenous context can impact an institution, as in the famous punctuated equilibrium model whereby radical institutional change occurs due to an exogenous shock (Baumgartner and Jones, 2009). Related to this is the notion of a "window of opportunity" for intentional institutional change, which could be a shock or simply other political factors such as electoral cycles, changes in discourse, public mood, and domestic and international events that create moments of attention (Sabatier, 2007). On the other hand, changes in context can also occur gradually, leading to slow-moving shifts, which may not appear to be causally significant for long stretches of time until a threshold is reached where a seemingly sudden effect appears (Pierson, 2004), for example, socioeconomic or demographic changes that play out over long timeframes leading to changes in political constituencies and preferences. Across levels of institutional order (e.g., programmatic, legislative, constitutional) institutions are likely to show different degrees of durability and persistence over time (Section 1.3). For example, programmatic institutions may permit change over relatively short timeframes (e.g., several years), legislative institutions may permit change over longer timeframes (e.g., years to decades), and constitutional institutions may only permit change over even longer timeframes (e.g., decades to centuries). Moreover, rules at one level can be seen as "nested" in deeper rules (Ostrom, 2005), which means that veto points or other forces of stability may be present at a deeper level than the level at which a particular change is sought. Yet scholars have recently argued that there is often much endogenous dynamism within institutions, which may not be immediately obvious, but which may permit ongoing gradual changes (Mahoney and Thelen, 2010). Yet this by no means implies complete flexibility for endogenous actors to reshape institutions, and they will often still be highly constrained. Altogether, this implies that even when subjected to pressures (Section 2.1), there are many reasons why institutions do not necessarily adjust accordingly.

2.3 Existing Theory on Institutional Change

Even though pressures on institutions do not automatically lead to institutional change, institutions *do* still change, sometimes intentionally and sometimes unintentionally. Indeed, the topic of institutional change has become prominent in recent years among not only institutional scholars (e.g., Mahoney and Thelen, 2010; Streeck and Thelen, 2005), but also sustainability scholars (Beunen and Patterson, 2019; Lorenzoni and Benson, 2014; Patterson et al., 2019; Young, 2010a). Therefore, in building a foundation for studying how institutions can be remade, it is important to first interrogate what is known about institutional change and its mechanisms more generally.

When examining institutional change, scholars commonly look to agency-structure interplay, that is, the ways in which certain actors exert influence on institutional structures, and the ways in which institutional structures shape and condition the actions of agents. Indeed, Goodin (1998) argues that the core argument of the overall "new institutionalist" paradigm, which emerged from approximately the 1980s onward in reaction to a behavioral paradigm,[14] is essentially "the recognition of the need to blend both agency and structure in any plausibly comprehensive explanation of social outcomes." This overall new institutionalist paradigm continues as the foundation of contemporary institutional analysis, albeit in a variety of guises emphasizing different causal features (e.g., rational choice, historical, sociological, discursive variants), both in political science generally (e.g., Hall, 2010; Hall and Taylor, 1996) and in sustainability (e.g., Betsill et al., 2020; Beunen and Patterson, 2019; Burch et al., 2019; Young et al., 2008). These various traditions suggest a variety of ways in which institutional change might occur (Table 2).

Of central importance across these traditions is the ways in which agents are presumed to behave. Historical institutionalism emphasizes contestation and conflict linked to power struggles, rational choice institutionalism emphasizes strategic behavior and coordination linked to calculation around self-interest, sociological institutionalism emphasizes culturally appropriate behavior linked to norms and practices, and discursive institutionalism emphasizes communicative behavior linked to reflexivity and deliberation. When it comes to thinking about attempts to (intentionally) remake institutions, all of these aspects are likely to be relevant. First, intentional change will inevitably be contested and trigger political struggles (historical institutionalism). Second, it will involve coordination around presumed joint interests to address a problem (rational choice institutionalism). Third, it will be driven at least partially by existing or changing norms and concerns over legitimacy (sociological institutionalism). Fourth, it will also be driven by deliberation among agents seeking to step outside of existing institutions and persuade others of the need for change (discursive institutionalism).

But all these behaviors occur within inherited institutional structures that constrain the range of possible action and the types of change that can be accomplished from one moment to the next. Institutions almost never provide a blank slate for action but carry legacies of rules, expectations, arrangements,

---

[14] Which itself was a reaction to a previous structure-focused paradigm, insightfully traced by Goodin (1998) in the same chapter.

Table 2 Implications about institutional change within core institutionalist approaches

Attribute	Institutionalism variant			
	Historical	**Rational choice**	**Sociological**	**Discursive**
Scale	Macro	Micro	Micro, Meso	Macro-Micro
Interactions	Conflictual	Coordinative	Cultural	Communicative
Presence of equilibria	No – Institutions are the outcome of historical processes	Yes – Benefit-seeking to optimize within structural contexts of rules	Partial – Cultural norms and values confer stability but are also fluid	Indeterminate – Discourses carry stability but can be challenged
Causes of institutional change	(i) Critical junctures, exogenous shocks (ii) Contestation over rules and their interpretation	(i) Shifts in external context (ii) Outcomes from previous "round" shape new setting	(i) Shifts in norms and legitimacy (ii) Changes in interpretations and/or practices	Agents act within and outside their institutions to persuade and influence others (Schmidt, 2008)
Timeframe	Gradual or rapid	Stepwise	Gradual	Sporadic

investments, and norms from prior moments. Even in cases where new institutions are created, this will probably not be in a vacuum but will be linked with existing institutions in some way, whether as a challenge to existing institutions or in some way connected to neighboring institutions. Hence, what matters for institutional remaking is understanding how agents are conditioned by institutional structures, at the same time as they act (for possibly multiple reasons) within these settings, and the overall consequences for (ongoing) institutional development over time.

In recent years, scholars have sought to theorize the mechanisms by which institutional change occurs. Past explanations of institutional change leaned particularly on exogenous factors under the punctuated equilibrium model, whereby periods of stasis are punctuated by moments of shock that trigger abrupt changes (Baumgartner and Jones, 2009). This is also reflected in the notion of critical junctures in historical institutionalism, where path dependency is redirected at key moments (often due to an exogenous shock). Among climate change scholars, it is sometimes suggested that climate-related disasters may provide "focusing events" (Birkland, 1998) capable of spurring political responses (e.g., Kates et al., 2012; Pralle, 2009). However, there may be no reason to expect that a crisis will automatically trigger reform due to a range of possible barriers to institutional change (Section 2.2).[15]

Contemporary political science shows skepticism toward exogenous factors as a sole explanation for institutional change. For example, Lieberman (2002, p. 697) argues that a "reliance on exogenous factors" limits a fuller understanding of institutional change. Instead, endogenous explanations of institutional change have been proposed, whereby institutions are seen to have the potential to change gradually as a result of ongoing political struggles over their meaning, interpretation, and enforcement, which introduces deviations that accumulate over time (Mahoney and Thelen, 2010; Streeck and Thelen, 2005). These scholars propose mechanisms of displacement (the introduction of new rules, which directly replace previous rules), layering (the introduction of new rules on top of or attached to existing rules), conversion (new interpretations or enactments of existing rules), and drift (the altered impact of rules within changing circumstances) (Mahoney and Thelen, 2010). The key insight here is to recognize that while the degrees of freedom available to agents are constrained in many ways, there are often also many ambiguities and openings present, which generate ongoing struggles and afford opportunities for flexibility (Mahoney and Thelen, 2010).

---

[15] Moreover, Weyland (2008, p. 285) suggests that arguments about crisis-driven reforms can be weak if made on functionalist grounds, although more convincing if made on cognitive-psychological grounds.

On the other hand, sustainability scholars often place significant emphasis on the relation between institutions and their exogenous context. For example, Young (2010a, 2010b) argues that institutional change in international environmental regimes is driven, to a significant extent, by pressure from environmental changes, mediated by the extent to which an institution is capable of managing the imposed stresses. This is suggested to occur through mechanisms such as market adjustment, learning, reauthorization of political authority, and amendment procedures (Young, 2010b). Broadly, this reflects a focus on the "fit" of institutions in their context. But such fit may not just involve material/environmental contexts, but also cognitive/discursive contexts, which are not necessarily aligned. This is especially relevant for climate change, where anticipatory action is grounded in knowledge and norms about unfolding and expected climatic shifts which have not yet (fully) manifested, at the same time that material climate impacts may also be occurring and stressing institutions in new ways.[16] In this light, Young (2013) identifies a need to integrate instrumental and interpretive explanations of institutional action, which also alludes to the relation between institutions and their ideational context (Lieberman, 2002; Patterson and Huitema, 2019).

More generally, Pierson (2004) emphasizes the need to pay attention to both short and long timeframes in examining mechanisms of institutional change, particularly due to threshold behavior, whereby slow-moving factors (e.g., socioeconomic or demographic shifts) go unnoticed until eventually producing a rapid change when a certain threshold is exceeded. This resonates with Young (2010a) in the environmental domain, considering the buildup of "stress" within institutions over time. As a result of slow-moving factors, "what may seem like a relatively rapid process of reform is in fact only the final stage of a process that has in fact been underway for an extended period" (Pierson, 2004, p. 141). This is relevant for climate change because slow-moving environmental shifts could cause institutional failures (Section 2.1). More subtly, various slow-moving socioeconomic and political factors could condition a society in ways that make institutional failure more or less likely under an abrupt climate impact. For example, growing social inequality, inadequate knowledge and preparedness, or erosion of political trust could raise the likelihood of catastrophic institutional failure under a major event such as a flood, drought, or storm.

Altogether, this suggests that understanding the (intentional) remaking of institutions requires considering both endogenous and exogenous factors and paying attention to unfolding processes of change over time. Attempts to

---

[16] This future-orientedness is a key challenge for the problem of remaking institutions (Section 1.5).

remake institutions are likely to be inherently political and, therefore, unable to be accomplished without work and struggle. For example, while some agents may seek to change institutions, others may react against changes by seeking to block or manipulate them (Capoccia, 2016), or to maintain existing institutions (Lawrence et al., 2009), or simply carry on with existing routines (Beunen and Patterson, 2019). Thus, institutional remaking will involve active "work" on the part of agents attempting to realize institutional changes. Mechanisms of institutional change are not likely to be straightforward or singular, especially for prospective (e.g., anticipatory) interventions, and may involve both instrumental and interpretive aspects. Moreover, we should expect that attempts to remake institutions will trigger complex political dynamics that play out against the backdrop of existing institutional orders within a particular social and material/environmental context.

3 The Notion of Institutional Remaking

Institutional remaking involves intentional activities undertaken by agents in light of institutional weaknesses or failures. Studying it requires adopting a processual perspective of politics, recognizing partial and unfolding action, and indeterminate and provisional outcomes. Intentionality is central but requires careful elaboration. Institutional remaking is distinct from typical notions of institutional design.

3.1 Defining Institutional Remaking

Institutional remaking is defined here as: *the activities by which agents intentionally develop political institutions in anticipation of, or in response to, institutional weaknesses and failures.* Hence, it is a political activity that seeks to influence certain type(s) of political institutions, motivated by experience or perceptions of institutional shortcomings. The term "remaking" encompasses both the "making" of new elements and the "remaking" of existing elements, while emphasizing that this (almost always) occurs within an existing (possibly already crowded) institutional setting. Thus, there is always a large degree of working with, and building on, what already exists, rather than the unproblematic introduction of new institutional designs.

Therefore, institutional remaking is distinguished from the notion of institutional design through an emphasis on unfolding processes, embeddedness, and political contestation. Yet it carries the same core interest in understanding how institutions may be intentionally improved. On the other hand, institutional remaking is a subset of the broader notion of institutional change, through its core focus on understanding activities that seek to intentionally bring about institutional change. The notion of institutional change encompasses a wider scope of interest in discovering and explaining processes of change occurring for all sorts of intentional and unintentional reasons. Hence, institutional remaking carves out a distinct focus combining the intentionality concern of institutional design scholars, with the process concern of institutional change (and especially institutional development) scholars. This is further discussed in Section 3.4.

Notably, the definition of institutional remaking proposed does not include a specific end or objective toward which institutional remaking is oriented. In the case of climate change and other pressing governance challenges (Section 1), institutional remaking is oriented toward improving the public good, where public good refers to ends which are, by some reasonable justification, aimed toward benefitting a broad public. This distinguishes institutional remaking from actions that are focused on advancing the private interests of a particular social actor only. Of course, there is no single public good in heterogeneous societies due to the presence of varying and even contradicting interests, preferences, and world-views. Nonetheless, as an intentional activity, institutional remaking is always done by certain social agents toward certain ends, which should be made explicit when studying it. The public good end is best defined with reference empirically to values and goals articulated by social actors within a given context.

Notably, by not pegging institutional remaking to a particular end, this allows it to be generalized as an analytical approach, which could also be applied to developments deemed negative by some social actors. For example, various political reform agendas favored by one political persuasion but disfavored by another could still readily be studied through a lens of institutional remaking. However, this is beyond the scope here.

3.2 A Processual Lens

The study of institutional remaking requires a processual lens focusing on the interactions by which institutional changes develop (or not). Of course, institutional scholarship contains rich processual insights and leanings, especially in lines of thinking on institutional development (Pierson, 2004, 2000a, 2000b, 1993) and comparative historical analysis (Mahoney and Thelen, 2015).[17] Elsewhere, much institutional scholarship focuses on static snapshots where initial and final states (e.g., State A, State B) take the foreground, and processes of change are secondary. However, studying institutional remaking requires embracing process as ontology, partly because of the inherently interactional and historically encumbered basis on which institutional changes develop, and partly because when we look forward in time we simply cannot know (or easily assume) what an end state (State B) may be, and therefore explaining change from State A to State B is difficult. We need to find ways to leverage existing insights about processes of institutional change (e.g., drawing on insights from rational, historical, sociological, and discursive lines of thinking; see Section 2.3), in an open-ended way looking forward in time.

Political institutions both cause and constitute struggles over climate change and societal transformation. Institutions are partially autonomous features of political life, which have casual influence on social and political activity but, at the same time, are themselves shaped by social and political activity (March and Olsen, 1983). Moreover, institutions involve inherent dynamism (Beunen and Patterson, 2019; Lawrence et al., 2009; Mahoney and Thelen, 2010), and their production and reproduction is "a dynamic political process" (Streeck and Thelen, 2005, p. 6) emerging from interactions among endogenous actors, and responses to exogenous circumstances.

---

[17] These lines of thinking are, in fact, central sources of inspiration for this Element.

Institutional remaking, in the fullest sense, is likely to often be an ongoing process, one that is "in-the-making" over extended timeframes and hence needs to be analyzed in ways that recognize this unfolding character. A key departure point is to move from a focus on institutional choice to a focus on institutional development: "To shift our focus from explaining *moments* of institutional choice to understanding *processes* of institutional development" (Pierson, 2004, p. 133, emphasis added). This is also important when treating institutional change as a dependent variable, where "established institutions modify the prospects for further institutional change" (Pierson, 2004, pp. 131–132).

However, sustainability scholars often treat institutions in a static way, as either inputs or outputs. As inputs, institutions are frequently invoked to explain performance failures in governance (e.g., success or failure of certain actions) or to explain difficulties in advancing climate change responses more generally (e.g., Biagini et al., 2014; Carter et al., 2015; Eakin and Lemos, 2010; Gupta et al., 2010). This approach treats institutions as an independent variable to explain other social, political, and environmental outcomes. As outputs, institutions are examined either in their actuality such as the institutionalization of new norms or practices (e.g., Anguelovski and Carmin, 2011; Aylett, 2015; Carmin et al., 2012) or in their ideal such as normative prescriptions concerning what "should" be implemented or changed in order to advance climate action. This is an approach that treats institutions as a dependent variable resulting from other causal forces. However, what is still missing is explicit theorization of the *processes of change* themselves. In other words, *institutional change* itself needs to be a dependent variable (following Mahoney and Thelen, 2010). This is crucial to understanding how existing institutions are, or could be, remade.

3.3 The Role of Intentionality

Until now, institutional remaking has been defined as an intentional activity. However, this warrants careful elaboration to situate the analytical role of intentionality. Potential pitfalls must be addressed regarding (i) the degree to which intentionality is possible given institutional complexity and (ii) whether or not functionalist arguments are invoked by the notion of institutional remaking.

First, intentionality captures the idea of actors attempting to address perceived institutional weaknesses or failures. On the one hand, it is clear that intentional institutional intervention is urgently required for problems such as climate change. Yet on the other hand, institutional intervention is notoriously challenging and plagued by unintended consequences (Goodin, 1998; Pierson, 2004, 2000b; Young et al., 2008). Institutions are typically encumbered by their past. For example, as Pierson (Pierson, 2000b, p. 493) observes: "Actors do not inherit a blank slate that they can remake at will when their preferences shift or unintended consequences become visible. Instead, actors find that the dead weight of previous institutional choices seriously limits their room to maneuver." Furthermore, societal heterogeneity means that consensus toward any particular course of action is unlikely. Thus, institutional remaking, concerned as it is with prospective changes, recognizes the need for intentionality but also its problems. How can this be reconciled?

The answer here is to relax the expectation that intentional intervention actually leads to the foreseen ends. The outcomes of institutional remaking will always depend on many factors within and outside the scope of control of any particular actor or coalition. However, the substantive problems at hand, and the desired directionality of improvement, nevertheless orient actions taken by actors. Moreover, it should not be expected that the goals of actors/ coalitions remain fixed. Negotiation and compromise, pragmatic judgments under bounded rationality, and difficulties realizing collective goals in practice may all modify the goals of actors attempting to remake institutions as these activities unfold over time.

Second, a more subtle, but potentially theoretically fraught (Pierson, 2000b) question arises about whether institutional remaking invokes functionalist arguments. Functionalism refers to a form of argumentation that "explains the origins of an institution largely in terms of the effects that follow from its existence. [however] ... [b]ecause unintended consequences are ubiquitous in the social world, one cannot safely deduce origins from consequence" (Hall and Taylor, 1996, p. 952). Functionalism would assume that pressures on institutions are acknowledged and addressed to enable a system to return to serving a predefined purpose. However, as has been previously noted, mechanisms such as learning, competition, and adaptation (which would be expected to kick in automatically under functionalism) are often likely to be weak (Section 2.2).

Pierson (2004) critiques both an "actor-centered functionalism" (which assumes that actors choose an institutional design in order to meet certain objectives) and a "societal functionalism" (which assumes institutional evolution through competitive selection driven by environmental pressures). While not denying their potential ubiquity, he argues that "they suggest a world of political institutions that is far more prone to efficiency and continuous refinement, far less encumbered by the preoccupations and mistakes of the past, than the world we actually inhabit" (Pierson, 2004, p. 131). Yet concerns about institutional weaknesses and failures may nonetheless motivate certain actors to attempt interventions, even while they are unable to escape the difficult realties of institutional politics (Section 2.2). The key point is that these motivations may not be singular or analytically sufficient for explanation. Doing away entirely with such reasoning obscures the potential to study intentional institutional changes at all (which indeed, some scholars may argue for). Yet this is exactly the challenge with which contemporary sustainability and political science scholarship must do better to engage with (Section 1.6). Moreover, there is no reason to assume that outcomes match objectives; the degree of "success" (however defined) can be assessed empirically.

Working with sustainability problems, such as climate change, raises murky questions about normative goals (and therefore assumed system purposes) and the relationship of institutions to their environmental contexts. For example, addressing climate change is, by definition, concerned with impacts and shifts in natural systems and their effects on human systems. This might make traditional institutional theorists wary of overreliance on functionalist argumentation. Sustainability scholars have approached this challenge through employing concepts such as the "fit" between human and natural systems (Young et al., 2008). For example, Young (2013, p. 91) contends that "the success of environmental and resource regimes is a function of the fit or match between the principal elements of these institutional arrangements and the major features of the biophysical and socioeconomic settings in which they operate." This helps to avoid function-alist oversimplifications by locating the degree of alignment between an institution and its context as an empirical question. It also connotes a problem-grounded focus, where a given sustainability governance problem must be recognized as embedded in both material/environmental and norma-tive (e.g., public good) contexts.

This can be further sharpened by considering the type of question being asked. When asking an ex post explanatory question, what matters is what *did* happen and how and why (hence excessive functionalism is a risk to construct-ing a valid or convincing explanation). However, when asking an exploratory question grounded in the present and with a view toward the future (which is a key focus when studying institutional remaking), then what matters is what *is* happening, and what *could* happen, and how and why (without presuming what outcomes might actually be produced). Arguably, if scholars are to put theory to work in helping to address pressing institutional problems, rather than wait for changes to play out in the world before venturing an explanation, then there is no choice but to engage with this murky middle ground.[18]

---

[18] This is certainly not to argue that sustainability governance scholars should become advocates. It is simply to recognize that helping to address societal problems involves engaging with real-world ambiguity and normativity in ways that are both exploratory and explanatory.

3.4 Design versus Remaking

Intentional intervention is often treated as institutional design and assumed to be rationally carried out toward instrumental ends. But there is no reason conceptually why institutional intervention cannot also be seen as an interpretive activity, conducted by actors toward their own (instrumental and interpretive) ends, within a particular context. This view of institutional intervention – as a contingent political activity with provisional and unfolding effects – remains undertheorized. This is the focus of institutional remaking.

Institutional remaking is centrally concerned with understanding the nature and effects of action on institutional structures, in other words, the *structural politics of institutional intervention*. It treats institutional intervention as an activity conducted over time and embedded within a certain context, rather than as a once-off moment. It also moves beyond seeing institutional intervention as an independent variable, either for explaining institutional performance or for prescribing the institutions needed to address certain problems effectively (e.g., Mitchell, 2006; Young et al., 2008). Instead, *institutional intervention itself becomes the dependent variable*. Sustainability scholars may be highly attuned to the challenges of institutional design: the fact that it can be imperfect, have unintended consequences, and by no means shows a direct relation with performance due to many other mediating factors (Young et al., 2008). For example, Young (Young, 2013, p. 102) reflects that "the establishment of any environmental governance system is an intensely political process in which interested parties struggle to promote their own preferences, often at the expense of the selection of options that would produce results that are more desirable in societal terms." However, there is still a so-far unaddressed need to break open the political dynamics of institutional intervention, recognized within a historical context but also with an explicit eye toward the future.

To do so, institutional remaking recognizes both activities and outcomes in a "comprehensive" approach (Section 4). Attempts to remake institutions may not have clear starting and stopping moments, and long-term problems are unlikely to be solved in a single moment but may instead involve ongoing jockeying and struggles. Indeed, Goodin (1998, p. 30) argues that analysts concerned with institutional design must begin with a notion of "design and *re*design, shaping and *re*shaping" (emphasis in original) because of the inevitable "backdrop of past practices" imposing "constraints and possibilities." Institutional remaking, therefore, directs attention to understanding activities playing out within what could be regarded as an "eternally unfolding present."[19]

---

[19] This term is drawn from Cook and Wagenaar (2012).

The term "remaking" itself has several helpful connotations. It implies a focus on ongoing activities (including work and struggle) rather than a single intervention moment, it directs attention to the *present* rather than only explaining the past (ex post) or seeking to predict the future (ex ante), it foregrounds the idea of beginning with existing institutional settings (which may be complex, crowded, and fragmented) rather than assuming a blank slate,[20] it suggests that both empirical analysis and normative judgments come into play, and most broadly, it reflects the long-standing notion that "effects becomes causes"[21] when analyzing institutions over time. It also permits consideration of ongoing/unfolding activities and partial/provisional outcomes. Overall, being grounded in a social production perspective (Section 1.5) leads to questions about how, why, and under which conditions institutional intervention arises and with what effects.

Nonetheless, some scholars are likely to be wary of studying institutional intervention, even when the focus is on endogenous agents taking this action, due to the role of intentionality. However, Goodin (1998, pp. 27–28) argues that intentional intervention does not necessarily mean linking any particular action to the realization of any specific outcome because unintended outcomes are ubiquitous, mistakes occur and no single agent determines outcomes. Furthermore, arguably, there are useful antecedents in institutional theory, which at least provide conceptual points of dialogue. For example, much institutional scholarship across the various institutionalisms (Section 2.3) now takes an agency turn, including in historical institutionalism where agency is posited as a key explanatory variable for institutional change (e.g., Capoccia, 2016; Mahoney and Thelen, 2010; Sheingate, 2014), in sociological institutionalism where "institutional work" seeks to explain diverse activities of agents within institutional settings (Lawrence et al., 2009), and in discursive institutionalism where agents step outside their institutionally defined roles to communicatively challenge dominant institutions (Schmidt, 2008). This interest in agency is certainly joined by sustainability scholars (e.g., Betsill et al., 2020; Beunen et al., 2017; Beunen and Patterson, 2019). While of course attention to agency does not equate with a focus on intentionality, it does suggest potential to explore institutional intervention as it is perceived by endogenous agents, which opens up the notion of institutional remaking.

---

[20] This also includes consideration of structures across levels. For example, examining how attempts to change a rule are, in turn, structured within a broader set of rules constraining how this may be done (Kingston and Caballero, 2009).

[21] Pierson (1993).

4 Observing Institutional Remaking

Finding ways to observe institutional remaking is vital for studying it empirically. Although given that institutional remaking encompasses both ongoing/
unfolding activities and partial/provisional outcomes, this is not straightforward. Observing institutional remaking entails both analytical and normative
judgments within a given context. A comprehensive frame, including evaluation categories, is needed.

4.1 Comprehensive Frame

Having defined institutional remaking in the previous section, the question
now arises: How can we know or evaluate when "successful" institutional
remaking has occurred? This is not a purely instrumental matter. Problems at
hand (such as climate change) are inherently political in their causes and
solutions, which therefore require assessing changes against instrumental and
normative criteria (e.g., some notion of the public good). Hence, observing
institutional remaking entails both instrumental and normative judgments,[22]
within a given context.

To speak of institutional "success" only makes sense in reference to some sort of
(explicit or assumed) purpose or functioning expected of an institution. For formal
political institutions[23] considered in the context of climate change, it is not an
unreasonable expectation that such a yardstick should often exist, even if
a particular institution in question serves multiple purposes (e.g., legislatures
making laws, upholding of property rights) or even is seen to serve different ends
by different actors (e.g., legal or policy obligations that require interpretation in their
enforcement). After all, whether political institutions are purposefully created at
a certain moment in time (e.g., laws, regulations, policies, political setups, coordination mechanisms), or arise in some other way (e.g., norms, practices), we typically
expect them to serve some sort of end in a democratic polity. Thus, in the context of
evaluation, it is not unreasonable to make judgments about institutional success,
either with reference to an institution's own implicit or stated purpose (e.g., to
achieve a democratically determined societal objective) or an external expectation
(e.g., protect human well-being and safety under climate change, ensure peaceful
resolution of conflict over resources in changing circumstances, reduce carbon

---

[22] Goodin (1998, p. 34) makes the observation that while normative aspects are clearly implied by
approaches focusing on institutional design, the link between empirical and normative aspects is
not typically explicated. In sustainability governance, Young et al. (2008) suggest that institutional design will be linked to both instrumental and normative factors.

[23] This is of course different for social institutions, which are likely to be much more emergent, and
thus any judgements about "success" are likely to be highly fraught with functionalist logic,
overly simplistic, and maybe even ethically inappropriate.

emissions). The challenge, though, is threefold (i) to avoid deferring to functionalist interpretations (e.g., institution X exists precisely *because* it serves a certain purpose), (ii) to avoid simplistic judgments about success without accounting for clusters of institutions (since no single institution is likely to be sufficient for addressing climate change in any of the ways identified in Section 1.1), and (iii) to avoid viewing success as a unanimously held view among social actors[24] (which would be unlikely under conditions of social heterogeneity).

Furthermore, institutional remaking is a processual phenomenon (Section 3.2), entailing both ongoing/unfolding activities and partial/provisional outcomes. Capturing such processes that are "in-the-making" is complex and may involve multiple criteria. For example, Goodin (1998, pp. 40–43) suggests several "middle-range" criteria for judging the success of institutional design: revisability balanced against productive stability, robustness and adaptability within changing environments, awareness of multiple motivations of agents, public reasoning and defensibility, and variability in the face of complexity. But we also need a way of comprehensively capturing both "movement" and tentative outcomes that may not have fully manifested. In essence, this reflects the challenge of *capturing an emergent trajectory as is it emerging.*[25] A comprehensive way of evaluating institutional remaking is therefore needed.

A novel starting point for a comprehensive approach to observing, and ultimately evaluating, institutional remaking is to draw on a line of thinking proposed by Amartya Sen in political philosophy about understanding progress toward enhancing justice in society (Sen, 2009). The underlying logic can be adapted to the challenge of institutional remaking for other contested and open-ended societal problems. Sen is concerned with practical social choice in settings involving incommensurable plurality of values. He argues that practical actions to bring about social improvement do not necessarily need to achieve, or even be oriented by, an "ideal" in order to be meaningful. Indeed, approaching the problem this way is likely to lead to gridlock given different preferences and values, he argues. Similarly, the ultimate end point of efforts to remake institutions for climate change (or other issues) is likely to be unclear at the outset, rendering ultimate consensus unlikely. Furthermore, institutional settings are

---

[24] For example, coastal retreat (i.e., deliberately moving built infrastructure away from coastlines vulnerable to climate impacts such as sea-level rise and storm surges) is increasingly discussed as a climate risk reduction strategy. However, it is unlikely that all involved social actors will share a common view about this. For example, Shi and Varuzzo (2020) find that property owners and even public authorities may oppose coastal retreat in the short term due to foregone property values and taxes, even if the same public authorities would benefit in the longer term from reduced risk exposure and legal and financial liabilities.

[25] For example, Stripple and Bulkeley (2019, p. 54) argue that, in the context of decarbonization, "[p]athways are the result of emergent processes as they realign and reorder socio-material relations in new sites and domains."

complex, and contexts change over time, meaning that it is unlikely that ideal institutions could ever be fully specified.[26]

Therefore, Sen (2009) advocates a need for "non-ideal" reasoning, in contrast to a "transcendental" reasoning that focuses on ideal arrangements. Nonideal reasoning starts with the empirical circumstances of the real world as it appears and tries to work out how to make improvements, rather than deriving prescriptions about ultimate goals from theory. Sen argues that this leads to a comparative approach, which may not be able to specify how a problem will be ultimately resolved but can nevertheless take feasible steps toward improving a situation from one moment to the next. This is profound because it liberates us from the expectation of knowing what ideal political institutions would look like before getting started. It also allows us to move away from "universal institutional designs and general 'solutions'" to instead "focus on the processes 'attuned to the suboptimal arrangements of an imperfect reality', a reality defined by abundant heterogeneity, diversity, and endemic disagreement" (Aligica, 2014, p. 25; quoting Rescher 1993). As a result, there is no need to assume that a single form or direction of institutional remaking is optimal.

Central to Sen's (2009) thinking is also the idea of "comprehensive" outcomes. This places a focus on jointly evaluating both the effects that result from social action and the processes by which they came about. Hence, it encompasses both consequentialist and deontic aspects; in other words, "what actually happens" as well as "how things are done" are part of the comprehensive outcome. This is important given the inherently political nature of institutional remaking and its scope encompassing both activities and outcomes. Attending to comprehensive outcomes helps to pay attention to both outcomes and the normative quality of activities undertaken.[27]

Together, the notions of nonideal reasoning and comprehensive outcomes provide a frame for observing institutional remaking. First, this focuses on feasible improvements rather than only on fully ideal solutions, which allows for identifying forms of institutional remaking that are, or could be, taken within actual institutional setups in a given moment. Second, it turns attention to comparative improvements both within and across cases (cross-sectionally and longitudinally). Third, it focuses attention on *trajectories* of institutional development as a basis for evaluating institutional remaking, for example, whether certain changes cumulate and have transformative effects. Fourth, it hints toward a need to recognize the capacity to produce institutional remaking on an ongoing basis.

---

[26] This point also follows from Mahoney and Thelen (2010).

[27] For example, considering democracy and legitimacy, however defined.

4.2 Evaluation Categories

Building on the previous section, three core evaluation categories for institutional remaking are: comparative improvement, directionality of institutional change, and the capacity for social action (Table 3). Comparative improvement focuses on finding feasible improvements compared to a prior or reference setting. Directionality of institutional change focuses on judgments about trajectories of institutional development. The capacity for social action focuses on the ongoing capacity to remake institutions over time.

"Comparative improvement" refers to substantive and feasible improvements within a given case. This involves assessing (possibly partial) outcomes of institutional remaking, such as institutional changes realized, or in progress. Indicators of comparative improvement may be endogenous to the case itself (i.e., longitudinal comparison across moments in time) or involve comparison with other relevant reference cases (i.e., cross-sectional or longitudinal comparison). In assessing comparative improvement there must be close attention to the specific details of a case, including the forms of institutional remaking that are (or could be) taken within the particular setting, context, and moment. Possible measures for comparative improvement may include material changes produced (e.g., emissions reductions),[28] preparedness for future expected conditions (e.g., climate adaptation), social outcomes (e.g., equity), legitimacy of activities, and the overall relationship between institutions and their context ("fit"). Empirically this might be observable as changes in institutions across various levels (e.g., programmatic, legislative, constitutional) or changes in various types of rules within a particular decision-making arena (e.g., relating to aspects such as boundaries, positions, choices, information, aggregation, payoffs, and scope).[29]

"Directionality of institutional change" refers to the trajectory of institutional development over time, as it is influenced by attempts to remake institutions within a given case. This involves judging the outcomes of institutional remaking against the extent to which the resulting institutional trajectory becomes better suited to addressing a particular problem (such as climate change), viewed within their historical context. This requires empirical and normative judgments. For example, a seemingly small change in a gridlocked setting might nevertheless be significant, and multiple small

---

[28] However, material emissions reductions are difficult to measure and attribute and may often be slow to change, even after institutional and political changes have occurred (e.g., Bulkeley et al., 2014, pp. 159–160). Thus, while this is central to problem-solving for climate change, it is an indirect and delayed measure of institutional remaking.

[29] Following Ostrom (2005); also applied to climate change adaptation by Patterson and Huitema (2019).

Table 3 Evaluation categories for institutional remaking

Category	Description	Indicators	Possible empirical measures	Indicator type
1. Comparative improvement	Substantive improvements within a given setting	i. Within-case problem solving ii. Between-case problem solving	• Emissions reductions • Risk reduction • Social equity • Legitimacy • Institutional "fit"	Comparative
2. Directionality of institutional change	Shaping the trajectory of institutional development	i. Immediate shifts ii. Shifts over time	• Radical institutional changes • Shifts in power and authority • Cumulative and catalytic effects	Temporal
3. Capacity for social action	Ongoing capacity to remake institutions over time	i. Capability ii. Durability	• Agency • Opportunity structures • Persistent changes in rules, with meaningful consequences	Generative

changes over time might cumulate into something more transformative, but this requires empirical judgment to determine. At the same time, the desirability of these changes must be judged against some sort of normative criteria (e.g., effectiveness, equity, efficiency). These judgments are challenging because shifts in institutional trajectories may be subtle or provisional and must be carefully interpreted.

Indicators of the directionality of institutional change may include (i) immediate shifts in institutional trajectories caused by institutional remaking and (ii) longer-term shifts in institutional trajectories triggered by a particular instance of institutional remaking (e.g., through cumulative and/or catalytic effects). Firstly, measures of immediate shifts (i) may include: radical institutional changes (relative to past institutional development) and institutional changes that significantly shift power and authority. Empirically, this might be observed as new ambitious goals, substantially altered behavior of public and private actors, and legal changes that change patterns of participation in political decision-making. For example, this could include legislation that mandates large-scale emissions reductions (e.g., ambitious targets for emissions reduction or renewable energy uptake), decommissioning of fossil fuel industries and frameworks supporting them (e.g., subsidies), incentivizing or sanctioning behaviors to stimulate low-carbon shifts, and legal changes to reflect climate risks (e.g., property rights, constitutions, standing). Secondly, measures of longer-term shifts (ii) may include cumulative effects and catalytic effects. Cumulative effects refer to temporal sequences whereby action in different institutional arenas or at different moments in time "join up" to produces substantial shifts in rules and/or patterns of political activity. For example, scholars sometimes suggest that incremental institutional changes can cumulate into transformative changes over time (Patterson et al., 2017; Streeck and Thelen, 2005). Empirically, this might be observed as a pattern of increasingly substantive actions that link and build up over time. For example, this could occur when certain impactful actions are observed to have only become possible because of earlier modest or tentative actions. This requires looking over an extended time period and at a system level in order to trace interdependencies between actions. Catalytic effects occur when action taken by "first movers" triggers action among actors who are otherwise reluctant, due to altered preferences (Hale, 2018). Indicators of catalytic effects include actions which trigger an increasing rate of change in rules and/or patterns of political activity. Empirically, this might be observed as changes in preference distributions (and subsequent actions) as a result of action taken by another actor or actions that involve "doing something differently to enable another entity to better perform a governance task" (Betsill et al., 2015).

"Capacity for social action" refers to the ongoing ability for actors to remake institutions over time. This involves assessing the factors underlying the production of institutional remaking. It is particularly important for evaluating institutional remaking as an unfolding activity without clear start and end points, which may play out over extended periods of time. Moreover, institutional contexts are always changing, particularly under climate change. Indicators of the production of social action are capability and durability. Measures of capability may include agency (of both individuals and coalitions) and opportunity structures. Empirically, this might be observed as the active creation and/or phase-out of certain systems. For example, this could include planning to decarbonize and adapt various sectors of society (such as energy, food, built environment, mobility, industry). Measures of durability may include changes in rules which "stick" over time and have meaningful consequences for political activity. Empirically, this might be observed as rules becoming accepted as legitimately "settled" matters even by opponents and changes in rules being further built upon both within a particular issue area (e.g., planning regulations about energy reduction in buildings being relied upon in national emissions reductions policies) and in other interlinked areas (e.g., introduction of low-emissions zones in cities spurring changes in future urban planning).

Altogether, these indicators and measures are by no means exhaustive and simply provide a starting point for evaluating institutional remaking. Nonetheless, the three core categories of Table 3 are arguably necessary to such an evaluation; in other words, they must all be present to meaningfully observe institutional remaking.

5 Political Dynamics in Institutional Remaking

Attempts to remake institutions are likely to involve contestation and struggle over institutional change in multiple areas. Disaggregating these political dynamics is important to provide tractable entry points for analysis. This is approached here by identifying five key "areas of institutional production" in which the politics of institutional remaking manifest:[30] novelty, uptake, dismantling, stability, and interplay. Each area of institutional production has been approached in a variety of ways in the literature, which is highly fragmented. The original synthesis here combines diverse insights to articulate key political dynamics of institutional remaking. This also helps to bring problem-focused sustainability scholarship into dialogue with broader institutional scholarship.

5.1 Overview

This section interrogates meso-level[31] political dynamics, which we would expect to play out during attempts to remake institutions, synthesized as areas of institutional production, namely novelty, uptake, dismantling, stability, and interplay. Together, this provides a heuristic typology (Table 4) and a set of entry points for empirical study, including the development and testing of hypotheses about institutional remaking. These five areas of institutional production coexist. Disaggregating them, therefore, is useful because institutional remaking may occur in several ways simultaneously. This opens up new opportunities to interrogate, theorize, and test the complex and interconnected political dynamics, which occur during attempts to remake institutions.

Importantly, the five areas of institutional production are all "positive" productions in the sense that they each contribute to actively shaping institutional development over time. This reflects a view of institutions as social phenomena that are continually produced and reproduced. For novelty and uptake this productive quality is intuitively clear. More subtly, stability is produced in the sense that underneath even seemingly stable and persistent institutions is often a foundation of continual dynamism (Section 2.3). However, even dismantling (which may at first glance sound de-productive) is actually a productive activity because it involves active work to bring about, and

---

[30] These categories are identified through synthesis of a broad range of theoretical and empirical scholarship (including climate change and environmental governance, sustainability transitions, political science, and sociology), where seemingly separate approaches can suggest common underlying concerns.

[31] As explained in Section 1.5, "meso-level" refers to a focus on rule clusters shaping collective decision-making arenas, in contrast to a micro-level perspective centering on individual actors, or a macro-level perspective centering on broad political structures and paradigms.

Table 4 Heuristic typology of political dynamics involved in institutional remaking

Category	Activity	Effect
Novelty	Introduction of new institutions (endogenous or exogenous sources)	Stimulating the use of new rules, norms, or practices
Uptake	Adoption and propagation of new institutions	Expanding and entrenching new rules, norms, or practices
Dismantling	Removal or destabilization of existing institutions	Diminished reach and influence of existing institutions
Stability	Conferral of continuity of existing institutions by political actors	Prevention or limitation on the adoption of new institutions
Interplay	Causally significant interactions with institutions in another domain	Conditioned or contingent institutional development

even if arising entirely due to neglect, such neglect is also ultimately a choice in some sense and therefore a productive action. Similarly, interplay is not an automatic property but rather one that is actively brought into being (e.g., cultivated, undermined, or both). This focus on "areas of production" reflects a processual ontology as articulated earlier (Section 3.2), as each of the five areas is something continuously unfolding and in-the-making.

5.2 Five Areas of Institutional Production

5.2.1 Novelty

Novelty refers to the introduction of new institutions, from either endogenous or exogenous sources, in order to enact or stimulate new rules, norms, or practices. Novel institutions are often intended to serve as prototypes or exemplars. The yardstick for viewing something as novel is related to the context in which it occurs. Sometimes, scholars argue that novelty does not need to be "new to the world," but rather, new to the context in which it is introduced, while others separate invention (i.e., novelty that is created from scratch) from diffusion (i.e., novelty that flows from one context to another) (Jordan and Huitema, 2014). In the approach developed here, novelty largely resonates with an invention perspective, but not so strictly that it must be entirely new to the world to qualify as such.[32] This is helpful because in an increasingly connected world, and in the face of an often non-infinite range of policy and institutional possibilities in real-world decision-making, it is too strict to limit the search for novelty to only the search for entirely fresh inventions. Taking seriously a rich view of context (e.g., comprising historical, political, social, and environmental dimensions) means that every context will be unique in many ways, and consequently novelty will be differently connected to different contexts. Of course, judgments about novelty are often a matter of degree and interpretation, in light of context.

Novelty of institutions is approached by scholars in several ways: (i) endogenous creation of new elements, (ii) changes in context which trigger novelty, and (iii) friction between institutional "orders."

Endogenous creation of new elements typically involves innovative or experimental institutional activity conducted by political actors within state or non-state arenas. This may involve innovative activity by state actors (e.g., Aylett, 2013; Hughes, 2017; Patterson and Huitema, 2019), viewing novelty through the lens of public value (Moore and Hartley, 2008; Wagenaar and Wood, 2018). It may also involve experimental activity extending beyond the state (e.g., civil society, business, and/or transnational actors) (e.g., Bulkeley and Castán Broto, 2013; Hoffmann, 2011), viewing novelty in terms of the extent to which it permits political actors to step outside the status quo (Farrelly and Brown, 2011; Frantzeskaki et al., 2016; Hoffmann, 2011). Sørensen (2017) notes three potential areas of novelty: innovations in polity (concerning authority over objectives and boundaries of decision-making), innovations in politics (concerning legitimate sources of authority for decision-making), and innovations in policy (concerning the formulation of policy programs). Often change agents figure prominently in explanations of novelty. For example, contemporary theory about gradual institutional change gives a prominent role to change agents, conditioned by their context, taking strategic action to press for changes in various ways (Mahoney and Thelen, 2010). Sustainability governance scholars also emphasize the importance of change agents in institutional innovation (Anguelovski and Carmin, 2011; Beunen and Patterson, 2019) and policy change (Brouwer and Huitema, 2017; Meijerink and Huitema, 2010). Importantly, the creation, promotion, and effects of novelty are inherently political (Jordan and Huitema, 2014). For example, Wagenaar and Wood (2018) argue that public innovation is better understood through a lens of contestation and democracy rather than managerialism and efficiency, because

---

[32] Furthermore, diffusion should arguably be circumscribed around a "tight" view of novel elements that are clearly mobile, in order to avoid concept stretching.

it involves social choice about the reconfiguration of relationships between state and non-state actors and ways of organizing, financing, and delivering public goods and services.

Changes in context triggering novelty can occur through shocks or through slow-moving shifts. In this view, the role of exogenous (rather than endogenous) factors is foregrounded, but what matters for institutional remaking is the influence of changes in context on the creation and sources of novelty, such as via change agents (Boin, 2005). Scholars have extensively highlighted the key role of context in triggering political dynamics (e.g., Falleti and Lynch, 2009; Ostrom, 2005). For example, Torrens et al. (2019) identify several ways in which context can condition the emergence of novelty, by shielding, facilitating, or provoking conflict around novelty. Context also affects whether or not novelty is accepted or "sticks." For example, Meijer et al. (2017) explore the conditions under which democratic innovations become durably connected to existing political arrangements. The role of shocks or crises in explaining moments of institutional change is extensively considered by institutional and policy scholars through a "punctuated-equilibrium" model (Section 4). While this model has come in for heavy criticism for downplaying dynamism in between shocks (Lieberman, 2002; Mahoney and Thelen, 2010), the role of disturbances remains significant under climate change because of the potential for climate impacts to act as focusing events for political activity (Birkland, 1998) or at least as causes of political conflict. On the other hand, Pierson (2004) emphasizes the importance of slow-moving causes, which accumulate stresses or erode the resilience of a system gradually leading to threshold effects (Section 4). In this way, slowly changing contexts may enable novelty through threshold behavior leading to moments of dramatic change.

Friction between institutional "orders" may give rise to new institutional configurations from existing ones through "intercurrence" (Lieberman, 2002; Sheingate, 2014). Intercurrence refers to the generative power produced by clashes between orders (Orren and Skowronek, 1996),[33] which permit or stimulate new configurations to form. Under this view, "institutional change occurs as the friction between orders generates incentives and opportunities for individual political action" (Sheingate, 2014, p. 464), through "dialectical tensions or conjuncture between multiple orders" (Sheingate, 2014, p. 470). Orren and Skowronek (1996) argue that intercurrence is a key source of change in political institutions over time. It is said to arise as a result of the inherent persistence of different orders within political life, which have developed for different reasons

---

[33] Where, again, orders are understood not as "orderliness" but as "the recognition of patterned regularity in social and political life" (following Lieberman, 2002).

and at different times, which means that "at any moment in time several different sets of rules and norms are likely to be operating simultaneously" (Orren and Skowronek, 1996, p. 111), "each with their own life history and logic" (Ethington and McDaniel, 2007, p. 139), thus creating "a political landscape riddled with incongruities and subject to continuous friction among its various components" (Orren and Skowronek, 1996, p. 112). Importantly though, "institutional politics is not in this view inherently conservative, resistant to 'forces of change,' or antithetical to creativity" (Orren and Skowronek, 1996, p. 140). Hence agency needs to be seen within a variegated institutional fabric that extends beyond any single set of rules and as centering on the reconfiguration of existing institutional elements in new ways rather than either the invention or import of new elements. It also suggests a degree of stochasticism in the appearance of novelty arising from clashes between "orders" that develop in different ways, over different timeframes, and for different reasons. Empirical examples could potentially be found in the recent proliferation of transnational climate governance arrangements and activities, which have developed over the last decade and which create new orders overlapping with those of state-centered global and domestic climate governance (e.g., Bulkeley et al., 2014; Chan et al., 2015; Hale, 2016).

5.2.2 Uptake

Uptake refers to the adoption and propagation of new institutional elements with the effect of expanding and entrenching these new elements. In other words, it is concerned with the mobility, reach, and effects of novelty. Uptake is studied through a variety of concepts and metaphors. For example, common notions include "diffusion," "scaling," and "institutionalization," among others. Yet all grapple with the underlying challenge of understanding how novelty moves and grows and ultimately comes to have broader effects within a system. Hence, the generic term "uptake" is used here to compare diverse insights that are typically considered separately. Political struggles over uptake occur in institutional remaking because new institutions are rarely taken up automatically, even in the presence of novelty. Active political work is needed to achieve this. Yet the dynamics of uptake remain poorly understood. While long a topic of interest, theorizing about uptake is lacking for institutional (cf. technological) novelty. This is now emerging at the forefront of sustainability governance, such as in climate governance (Bernstein and Hoffmann, 2019), sustainability transitions (Turnheim et al., 2020), and urban governance (Peng and Bai, 2018).

Uptake of new institutions is approached by scholars in a variety of ways: (i) expansion of new elements, (ii) self-reinforcing feedback, and (iii) systemic effects.

Expansion of new elements is typically viewed as a process of outward, upward, or inward expansion. First, the outward expansion of novelty ("horizontal" expansion) from one site to another is commonly approached as diffusion. Scholars examine mechanisms such as replication, competition, bandwagoning, strategic dissemination, and learning (Jordan and Huitema, 2014; Shipan and Volden, 2012; Strang and Soule, 1998). Yet diffusion typically envisions novelty as a portable product (e.g., technologies, policy interventions), underplaying deep constitutive ties between novelty and context. Second, the upward expansion of novelty ("vertical" expansion) from one level to another is commonly approached as escalation. Scholars examine "strategic niche management" as a technique to drive the escalation of novelty (Schot and Geels, 2008) and reflexive practices that stimulate learning in governance thereby helping to take up novelty (Loorbach, 2010; Turnheim et al., 2015). However, specific causal mechanisms of escalation remain under-theorized, beyond a general expectation that they will occur under certain circumstances such as successful experimentation. Third, the embedding of novelty ("inward" expansion) within an existing institutional setting is commonly discussed as institutionalization. Scholars examine mechanisms by which new rules, practices, and norms are absorbed into an existing institutional fabric with the effect of simultaneously changing this fabric (e.g., Anguelovski and Carmin, 2011; Aylett, 2015). This implies that prevailing norms are both accommodated and reshaped. Relatedly, Patterson and Huitema (2019) argue that embedding of institutional novelty depends on interactions between rules and underlying "governance dilemmas," implying that the uptake of novelty is unlikely if it does not align with (or realign) core problem frames.

Self-reinforcing feedback refers to political effects produced by institutions/ policies whereby institutions/policies amplify the conditions supporting their own enactment and dominance over time. This is a form of positive feedback *following* the introduction of an institutional element,[34] which occurs through the gradual reshaping of incentives, interests, and capacities of political actors (Jacobs and Weaver, 2015, p. 443). Pierson (2004, 2000a) emphasizes the role of self-reinforcing feedback through the notion of "increasing returns" as a mechanism of path dependency (Section 2.2). But it is also a potential mechanism of uptake, whereby the dominance of a new institutional element not only persists, but increases, over time. Such a view directs attention to the ways in which a new institution is capable of shifting incentives, interests, and capacities. Some scholars have taken up such thinking by examining how

---

[34] In contrast to positive feedback that may build up *prior to* an institutional or policy change, which has the effect of stimulating such a change (Jacobs and Weaver, 2015, p. 443).

positive feedback may be anticipated in order to achieve durable policy design. For example, Jordan and Matt (2014) explore the potential for climate policy to have "opportunity enhancing" effects that could increase its propensity to "stick" once introduced. Yet starting conditions are also likely to matter. For example, Maltzman and Shipan (2008) explore how political conditions at the time of legislative enactment influence the chance of institutional revision down the track. Altogether, this directs attention to the temporal dynamics by which uptake (in the sense of durability and dominance of a new institution) may occur.

Systemic effects refer to patterns of structural change within a (complex) institutional arena. This is similar to, but distinct from, self-reinforcing feedback. Systemic effects involve the reconfiguration of rules due to the interaction of multiple sources of novelty and/or shifts in context, whereas self-reinforcing feedback focus on the political effects produced by a particular institutional change. At the same time, systemic effects do not assume feedback per se but focus on interactions between multiple sources of novelty (e.g., cumulative effects, catalytic effects) and/or interactions between novelty and changing contexts (e.g., threshold effects). Cumulative effects have been proposed as a way in which many incremental institutional changes may, combined, bring about transformative shifts (Streeck and Thelen, 2005). This could be highly relevant to institutional remaking, because, as Sheingate (2014, p. 469) points out, "whereas frontal assaults on core institutions will often provoke staunch resistance, incremental change at the margins may occur virtually unnoticed or be sold as minor correctives or repairs to existing institutions." Catalytic effects are a newer topic of interest among climate governance scholars, whereby the interests and preferences of political are understood to be at least partly determined by actions already taken by other actors, rather than static and prefixed, which creates the possibility for action to generate further action over time (Hale, 2018). For example, Bernstein and Hoffman (2018b, p. 191) suggest that subnational experiments may have catalytic political effects "by altering political dynamics within and across jurisdictions, markets, and/or carbon-intensive practices." This is relevant to institutional remaking because it directs attention to the potential catalytic role of specific institutional changes. Threshold effects refer to major changes which seem to appear abruptly but are actually the consequence of slow-moving causes building up over long timeframes that reach a tipping point (Pierson, 2004). For example, Jacobs and Weaver (2015, p. 451) argue that windows of opportunity (in the punctuated equilibrium model) often only arise because of "much longer-term processes that have reshaped the underlying distribution of interests and policy preferences among elites and the mass public." This alerts attention not only to the possibility of sudden uptake of new institutions, but also to the importance of considering small shifts, which may seem inconsequential at any given moment in time, but which may be consequential over longer timeframes. Nonetheless, anticipating threshold effects in politics is likely to be extremely difficult looking forward in time. Thus, the main role of threshold effects may be simply to sensitize analysis to the potential significance of slow-moving changes and to continually call into question assumptions about the stability of incumbent institutions.

5.2.3 Dismantling

Dismantling refers to the removal or destabilization of existing institutions leading to them having diminished reach and influence. This is a relatively new area of thinking, both in sustainability governance and in broader political science. Yet it is vital for understanding how space may be created for novelty and its uptake within often crowded institutional settings. Furthermore, the politics of dismantling are likely to be equally as challenging as the politics of uptake and might include battles over shifts in powers, resources, and positions of incumbents (Brisbois, 2019; Roberts et al., 2018). For example, Patashnik (2014, p. 5) argues that policy reform is not only a matter of assembling new elements, but crucially, "some extant policy system must be cleared away or at least contained before a reform can be safely established." Dismantling of institutions to promote climate change action might include the removal of subsidies and arrangements which support fossil fuel production systems (Skovgaard and van Asselt, 2019), modification of policies and laws that sustain the use of carbon-intensive technologies (e.g., for energy, mobility, food), modifying property rights that prove to be incompatible with new climate conditions (e.g., water rights, land title),[35] and weakening arrangements and/or venues that give incumbent actors disproportionate influence in political decision-making (e.g., corporate lobbying). Scholars increasingly call attention to the issue of dismantling in sustainability governance (Abson et al., 2017; Newig et al., 2019), sustainability transitions (Geels, 2014; Loorbach et al., 2017; Turnheim and Geels, 2012), and policy studies (Jordan et al., 2013).

Dismantling of institutions is approached by scholars in a variety of ways: (i) strategic dismantling by political actors and coalitions, (ii) self-undermining feedback, and (iii) abandonment.

---

[35] Such as in risk-prone areas for floods or sea-level rise (Freudenberger and Miller, 2010; McGuire, 2019).

Strategic dismantling by political actors and coalitions encompasses deliberate efforts to remove or destabilize existing institutions that are viewed as barriers to the introduction and use of new institutional elements. Strategic dismantling can focus on instrumental aspects (such as rules themselves), although within heterogeneous settings analysts need to be clear about "*which* costs and benefits are at issue*" (Jordan et al., 2013, p. 797) and to whom, because dismantling can be pursued by different actors for different ends. Strategic dismantling can also focus on interpretive aspects (such as meaning and symbols), because certain problem frames may reinforce an existing set of rules, or conversely, undermine them.[36] For example, policy scholars have observed rule dismantling by change agents as part of broader political agendas toward deregulation over recent decades (Jordan et al., 2013). These scholars tend to approach dismantling through a lens of bureaucratic politics (e.g., strategic decision-making by political elites, blame avoidance, agenda-setting, and redistributive politics). Interestingly, they suggest that dismantling can trigger the mobilization of coalitions seeking to gain certain benefits, as well as anti-dismantling coalitions (Jordan et al., 2013). Sustainability transitions scholars have also emphasized the role of the state in conducting dismantling, because the rapid phasing out of particular industries (or at least support for them) can seemingly only be achieved while working through state institutions and may also require intervention in markets (Johnstone and Newell, 2018). Elsewhere, organizational scholars have emphasized the importance of disruption by endogenous political actors as a key form of "institutional work" involved in institutional change (Lawrence et al., 2009). Such disruption may include withholding certain actions such as the application of sanctions or even questioning the legitimacy of existing arrangements (Lawrence et al., 2009). While the notion of institutional work has been explored in sustainability governance (Beunen et al., 2017; Beunen and Patterson, 2019; Brown et al., 2013), understanding the ways by which strategic disruption is undertaken remains vastly underdeveloped.

Self-undermining feedback refers to political effects produced by institutions/ policies whereby institutions/policies undermine the conditions supporting their own durability and persistence over time. This is a form of long-term negative feedback following the introduction of an institution/policy,[37] which leads to

---

[36] For example, whether climate change is seen as a burden-sharing problem in society or as an opportunity for social and economic development (e.g., as promoted by a "Green New Deal" approach).

[37] This applies the idea of negative feedback – that is, a system property whereby an effect produced under certain conditions undermines the conditions that give rise to it, thus in turn weakening the effect over time (Jordan and Matt, 2014) – to studying the effects of policy intervention over time.

"policy rollback or reorientation" (Jacobs and Weaver, 2015, p. 443). This is suggested to occur through a variety of possible mechanisms, including "the emergence of unanticipated losses for mobilized social interests," "interactions between strategic elites and loss-averse voters," and "expansions of the menu of policy alternatives" (Jacobs and Weaver, 2015, pp. 444–450). From another angle, Patashnik (2014) examines the post-adoption dynamics of policy reforms in the United States, arguing that political struggles over reform require ongoing effort to reconfigure policy systems far beyond the formal enactment phase of a reform, without which reforms can turn out to be much less impactful and enduring. Yet overall, self-undermining feedback is an area that is only beginning to be studied.

Abandonment refers to the conscious or de facto cessation in the application of certain institutions. This is a topic that is rarely studied, although is emerging as an area of interest from different angles. On the one hand, institutional change theorists have posited a mode of "drift" whereby existing institutions remain unadapted within changing circumstances, rendering their impact diminished or dysfunctional over time (Mahoney and Thelen, 2010). Diminished impact could lead to the de facto abandonment of no-longer helpful institutions, and dysfunctional impact could stimulate conscious cessation. Relatedly, Sheingate (2014, p. 469) observes that "the creation of novel institutional arrangements alongside existing ones can siphon off support of key constituencies or assume a more prominent role in guiding behavior," thus potentially leading to the stagnation of institutions left behind or possibly creating imperatives to transform them. From a policy angle, Patashnik (2014) examines "slippage" between the actions of governmental actors and the preferences and interests of citizens, which could sometimes conceivably entail covert abandonment of certain institutions by bureaucrats or elected officials. However, the conditions under which institutions are abandoned, rather than actively dismantled, remain unclear.

5.2.4 Stability

Stability refers to the ways in which the continuity of existing institutions is conferred by political actors, with the effect of preventing or limiting the adoption of new institutions. Stability is increasingly viewed as a property that is actively produced and reproduced, rather than something that is predetermined or fixed (e.g., Beunen and Patterson, 2019; Patterson, 2019). This is not to say that stability is easy to overcome, but such a view focuses on examining dynamism in the sources of stability and its production over time. Problematizing stability raises curious tensions because institutions, by definition, produce regularity in social interactions, which can be desirable and important for political affairs, yet may sometimes also be problematic and create barriers to important institutional changes that are understood to be needed (Beunen et al., 2017). For example, at the broadest level, stable institutions supporting democratic accountability and the rule of law are foundational in liberal democratic societies. Institutions that are actively set up to support social equity (e.g., concerning health, welfare, finance) may need to remain in place over long timeframes to be effective, since issues of socioeconomic underdevelopment and economic inequality often need long-term intervention. Businesses typically require stable rules to provide certainty for their planning and investment. Therefore, institutions that change too frequently may risk undermining confidence, trust, and even legitimacy. Efforts to remake institutions for addressing climate change need to consider both "productive" or desirable sources of stability, as well as those which are problematic.

Stability of institutions is approached by scholars in a variety of ways: (i) system persistence, (ii) active resistance, and (iii) maintenance.

System persistence refers to the ways in which existing institutions tend to remain dominant and reproduce over time. This is caused by factors such as path dependency, inefficient mechanisms of change, constraints linked to material contexts, and weak opportunity structures permitting change (See Section 2.2). Institutional scholars have emphasized the role of path dependency produced through increasing returns dynamics (Section 2.2). Such dynamics arise from the material and interpretive effects of existing institutions/policies over time, which tend to reinforce the resources, expectations, powers, and cognitive schemas benefitting actors in incumbent positions (Pierson, 2004, 2000a, 1993). Sustainability scholars have emphasized the role of "lock-in," especially the notion of "carbon lock-in" (Unruh, 2002, 2000), where interconnected subsystems mutually reinforce each other, preventing changes being realized in any individual subsystem. For example, Seto et al. (2016) identify three key sources of carbon lock-in relating to infrastructure and technology, institutional setups, and behaviors and practices, which mutually reinforce each other and make it difficult to realize changes in any individual area alone. Such issues of lock-in confront efforts to remake institutions, because of the deep embeddedness of carbon in the political economy (Newell and Paterson, 2010; Raworth, 2017) and even the culture (Bulkeley et al., 2016; Feola et al., 2019) of industrial societies. Bernstein and Hoffman (2018b) argue that a key task, therefore, is to find ways to "unlock" lock-in, with promise lying in "diverse, decentralized responses" such as actions of subnational actors in climate change governance. This resonates somewhat with insights from institutional scholarship where Pierson (2004, p. 142) argues that "the successful generation of grievances against particular institutional arrangements must be understood as partly a breakdown on the factors reinforcing the status quo," thus directing attention to understanding the factors supporting the status quo and the conditions under which their strength breaks down. Yet Thelen (1999, p. 396) cautions that the metaphor of lock-in, depending on how it is conceived, can underplay the political factors involved in realizing institutional persistence. Usefully though, an examination of system persistence through a (political) perspective of lock-in can broaden consideration beyond institutional factors (as suggested by path dependence) and also direct attention to the role of materiality (e.g., infrastructures, technology, behaviors/practices) in stabilizing institutions.

Active resistance refers to deliberate efforts taken by political actors to block changes to existing institutions. For example, Pierson (2004, p. 141) argues that "understanding the preconditions for particular types of institutional change requires attentiveness not only to the pressures for reform but also to the character and extent of *resistance* to such pressures" (italics in original). For example, in the context of climate change, Lockwood et al. (2017) observe how incumbents in the UK electricity sector have guarded against change through capturing rule-making power by leveraging self-governance arrangements concerning key technical and commercial matters. Resistance by incumbents (e.g., energy utilities, corporations, government authorities) is a widely adopted explanation for the stability of existing systems among sustainability scholars (e.g., Brisbois, 2019; Geels, 2014; Scoones et al., 2015). Examining sources of resistance involves considering the mobilization of political actors and coalitions, as well as opportunity structures for veto (Lockwood et al., 2017; Pierson, 2004; Tsebelis, 2002). Capoccia (2016) takes up this issue, arguing that veto points are not static and require close attention to the ways in which certain actors "slow down, channel, or stop change" (p. 1117). Capoccia (2016) argues that this can occur through the institutionalization of cultural categories (e.g., the reification of certain norms and values by ongoing policy choices) and/or the ability of incumbents to exercise power over the nature and timing of reforms, both of which give opportunity to incumbents to impede changes. Overall, the dynamics of agency resisting institutional change is an area requiring greater attention across diverse domains of sustainability governance (Patterson, 2019).

Maintenance refers to "everyday" actions taken by diffuse actors within an institutional setting to consciously or unconsciously reproduce the stability of existing arrangements. This encompasses practices, habits, and routines and therefore implies a key role for sociological aspects such as beliefs and culture (Patterson and Beunen, 2019). Maintenance differs from system persistence by emphasizing everyday activities rather than wider system change/stability and differs from active resistance, in emphasizing sources of institutional stability arising from endogenous but dispersed actors who are also not typically considered as change agents. The institutionalization of cultural categories (Capoccia, 2016) is also relevant to maintenance in terms of influencing the behavior of dispersed actors within an institutional arena (e.g., bureaucrats and decision-makers), whose actions are shaped by the delineation of cultural categories, which they themselves may lack control over. Importantly, maintenance can underpin both "productive" institutional stability, as well as obstructive stability against desired institutional change. As mentioned previously, maintenance of many institutions is required on an ongoing basis (e.g., for democratic accountability, rule of law, long-term policy programs, business confidence). A lack of maintenance can undermine the stability of such institutions/policies. For example, Chapron et al. (2017) recently observed a trend that multiple governments around the world are failing to maintain their own biodiversity policies, threatening institutional stability in this domain. Maintenance also raises questions about the causes of actors' behaviors. For example, maintenance could be driven by a sense of duty or consequence, belief in dominant schemas or imaginaries, perceptions of low power to effect change, or avoidance of discomfort or the risk of drawing attention. On the other hand, maintenance could relate to a tendency toward isomorphism in organizations, whereby actors seek to legitimate their activities with reference to prevailing norms, stabilizing an existing system against novelty, even though they may ostensibly call for novelty (DiMaggio and Powell, 1983). A focus on maintenance therefore encompasses both micro- and macro-dynamics of institutions, as they come together in meso-level institutional arenas. Yet maintenance, so far, seems vastly understudied in sustainability governance.

5.2.5 Interplay

Interplay refers to interactions between institutions in a particular domain with those in another domain, which are causally significant for patterns of institutional development. Institutional remaking can be conditioned by, contingent on, or impactful for institutions in other linked domains. Interplay therefore focuses on interactions between institutions across multiple arenas or domains, which differ from lock-in (a form of stability), which focuses on interactions with material and behavioral aspects. Interplay is important to consider because institutional settings relating to climate change within the domestic political sphere will often be densely packed, since climate change governance is connected to many other areas of political activity (e.g., energy, health, food, mobility, cities, waste). Interplay will therefore be inescapable in complex institutional settings, where the success of institutional remaking will depend on trans-sectoral institutional linkages. The general insight that "changes in one institutional arena can reverberate, provoking changes in other, complementary institutions" (Thelen, 1999, p. 396), is salient. Consequences of interplay may be "beneficial, adverse, or neutral for the target institution" (Oberthür and Gehring, 2006a, p. 4). For example, scholars examining fragmentation in global governance have identified synergistic, cooperative, and conflictive forms of institutional interaction (Biermann et al., 2009). Others examining "polycentric" patterns of climate governance[38] point toward forms of interplay arising through competition, coordination, or mutual adjustment (Jordan et al., 2018). On the whole, institutional interplay has been studied at a global level in terms of interactions between institutional regimes (e.g., Oberthür and Stokke, 2011; van Asselt, 2014; Young et al., 2008), whereas in the domestic sphere similar issues are often approached through a lens of policy integration (e.g., Jordan and Lenschow, 2010; Tosun and Lang, 2017).

Getting a grasp on interplay is not straightforward, and a variety of conceptual lenses have been proposed. A common distinction is that of horizontal and vertical interplay (Young et al., 2008), where horizontal interplay looks across domains at a certain level of organization, and vertical interplay looks across scales. Young (2002) argues that such interplay occurs through both functional modes (i.e., due to substantive problem overlaps) and strategic-political modes (i.e., deliberate management). Concerning international environmental regimes, Oberthur and Gehring (2006a) identify four mechanisms of interplay relating to cognitive aspects (involving persuasion and learning), commitments (involving preferences in light of other institutions), behavior (involving behavioral changes caused by other institutions), and impacts (involving overlapping outcomes of concern). Within the domestic sphere, Jordan and Lenschow (2010) identify key classes of factors influencing policy integration, namely coordination mechanisms built into institutions (e.g., "soft" approaches such as budgets and financing, and "hard" approaches such as inter-ministerial coordination), political behavior (e.g., hierarchical leadership, zones of authority), and cognitive frameworks (e.g., administrative traditions, routines, preferences). More generally, Tosun and Lang (2017) point to two key variables in policy integration: sources of interdependence between policies and degree of cooperation between involved actors. These various approaches have relevance to institutional remaking, but all are motivated by an underlying concern for institutional performance. Since institutional remaking is a processual phenomenon with often partial or provisional outcomes (Section 3), what is needed is to

---

[38] Polycentricity refers to governance systems with many dispersed centers of authority that are autonomous but also interdependent, following V. Ostrom et al. (1961), and Jordan et al. (2018).

examine the ways in which interplay may support or hinder institutional remaking or co-develop over time.

Interplay can therefore be approached from several angles: (i) linkage/synergy, (ii) conflict/tension, and (iii) co-development.

Linkage/synergy refers to the range of structural and agential mechanisms by which institutions that are remade in a particular arena are supported and reinforced by institutions in other arenas. For example, in the international sphere, Oberthür and Gehring (2006b) propose a notion of "interplay management" as the deliberate political work undertaken by endogenous actors (e.g., bureaucrats, policymakers) to manage and improve interaction between institutional regimes. This may include regulatory activities (e.g., concerning permitted and sanctioned behaviors) and enabling activities (e.g., concerning communication and learning) (Oberthür, 2016). Relatedly, in the domestic sphere, Tosun and Lang (2017, p. 557) observe that moves toward "policy coherence" require both "institutions that facilitate the integration process" as well as "cooperation and political leadership." Importantly, Oberthür (2016) points out that (deliberate) interplay management can typically only be accomplished on an incremental basis, rather than through radical reforms due not only to the difficulty of achieving radical reforms, but also the pragmatic need to build on existing structures. On the other hand, scholars have explored whether subsystems within a polycentric order show mutual adjustment in an at least partly spontaneous fashion, observing that proactive national climate policy settings can influence the propensity for domestic actors to organize in the transnational sphere (Jordan et al., 2018). Yet given a view of political institutions as inefficient in adjusting to change (Section 2.2), embodied by agents (Section 2.3), and often contested on an ongoing basis (Section 2.3), spontaneity may only be a useful frame when investigating at a system level. Yet the notion of mutual adjustment seen as a political activity (e.g., linked to structures requiring interaction, or agents choosing to cooperate) remains salient and may be a useful lens to apply to institutional remaking, as it does not expect any specific "work" on the part of agents involved, but instead makes this an empirical question.

Conflict/tension refers to the range of structural and agential mechanisms by which institutions that are remade in a particular arena conflict or compete with institutions in other arenas. For example, sustainability scholars examining fragmentation in global governance identify the potential for conflictive interplay caused by both strategic factors (i.e., where political actors come down on either side of conflicting arrangements) and normative factors (i.e., due to conflicting core norms) (Biermann et al., 2009). More broadly, in the sphere of transnational governance, Blome et al. (2016, p. 4) observe that conflict may arise not only from contradictory rules across overlapping regimes concerning a particular policy or legal issue, but also because of contradictory "society-wide institutionalized rationalities, which law cannot solve." This suggests that both deeply held norms and historical patterns of institutional development surrounding a particular institutional arena have potential to produce conflict, as well as from particular policies or institutional elements. On the other hand, such clashes could sometimes be generative. For example, Lieberman (2002) argues for a view where political change "arises out of 'friction' among mismatched institutional and ideational patterns" (p. 697), where clashes between previously stable patterns can render the continuation of normal activities difficult, exposing disjuncture between different ideas and inducing political actors to "find new ways to define and advance their aims" (p. 704) in different institutional forums or by aligning with new opportunities. Lieberman (2002) suggests that this results in the reconfiguration of institutional elements rather than their wholesale replacement. For institutional remaking, this indicates that tension/conflict may not always be constraining, although it may well be volatile. Broadly, this reflects a (conflictual) developmental perspective, where new expressions of institutional order are created from a different configuration of elements.

Co-development refers to ways in which institutional remaking in a particular arena influences a separate but linked arena, which in turn influences the original arena. This process of shaping and reshaping plays out over time. It could occur through mutual adjustments that advance synergies or through reconfiguration triggered by conflict. Hence, rather than being entirely distinct from the subcategories mentioned earlier, co-development may involve aspects of both linkage/synergy and tension/conflict. Importantly though, mutual causal influence is an important characteristic of co-development: "Two or more institutions may 'co-evolve' over time with influence running back and forth between the institutions so that neither of the institutions would exist in its current state in the absence of the other" (Oberthür and Gehring, 2006a, p. 4). Institutional arenas could converge or diverge over time. A common approach to envisioning linkages across arenas in the sustainability literature is the notion of boundary spanning (Cash et al., 2003). From a policy studies perspective, Tosun and Lang (2017, p. 560) suggest that the success/development of boundary spanning is influenced by whether subsystems are tightly coupled (which promotes "serial" processing of issues, and therefore convergence over time) or loosely coupled (which promotes "parallel" processing of issues, and therefore divergence over time), the extent of agreement between actors in different subsystems, and the extent of agreement different concerned publics. More broadly, the notion of coevolution is employed by some sustainability scholars, such as in sustainability transitions studies (van den Bergh et al., 2011) and institutional economics (Kallis and Norgaard, 2010; van den Bergh, 2007). While this notion usefully captures the idea of interactive developments at the level of metaphor, it is difficult to apply analytically to political institutions because it often leans on Darwinian notions of variation, selection, and inheritance (Kallis and Norgaard, 2010). As discussed in Section 2.2, adjustment in political institutions is typically inefficient, adjustment is not subject to classical mechanisms of competition and selection because institutional choice is heavily weighted by the past and activity may occur under monopoly of a single institutional arena, competition does not happen on a neutral slate because political institutions provide both the arena for political struggles as well as the prize of it, and many institutional choices are "once-off" and not subjected to repeat competition (at least in the same form). Thus, the notion of co-development better captures the effects of political struggles relating to interplay over time, as well as allowing the possibility to capture broader interactive developments affecting institutional remaking in a particular domain.

5.3 Synthesis

The five areas of institutional production identified – *novelty, uptake, dismantling, stability,* and *interplay* – together provide a comprehensive lens for analyzing institutional remaking. Each of these areas of production is likely to play out individually, but they may also interact, such as occurring simultaneously or in sequence. For example, uptake and dismantling may occur sequentially: Dismantling may need to occur first to make space for uptake of new institutions, or uptake may need to occur first to stimulate dismantling. Both uptake and dismantling are in tension with stability.[39] Novelty and uptake may occur sequentially as novel institutional elements stimulate uptake. Stability and interplay may be interdependent: Linkages with institutions in another domain may stabilize the rules of a particular decision-making arena, or on the other hand, changes in institutions in another domain may undermine stability of a particular decision-making arena. Hence, in their fullest sense, the five areas of institutional production need to be considered jointly as well as individually.

Yet each individual area of institutional production is itself complex and potentially multi-causal. A key benefit of the typology is that it opens up new opportunities to develop precise causal mechanisms involved in institutional

---

[39] For example, "understanding the preconditions for particular types of institutional change requires attentiveness not only to the pressures for reform but also to the character and extent of *resistance* to such pressures" (Pierson, 2004, p. 141, italics in original).

remaking, within a broader perspective. In Sections 5.2.1–5.2.5, the five areas of institutional production have been decomposed, showing various ways in which they are approached in current literature. While this does not in itself provide testable causal mechanisms, it directs attention to key causal features that can be used to develop such explanations. Table 5 summarizes the five areas of institutional production, also identifying the causal features indicated by each, which provides a basis for hypothesis generation and testing. Notably, hypotheses can be limited to interrogating causality within any individual area, or they can consider various permutations (e.g., to explore interactive effects such as simultaneous presence, sequential dependence, or conditioning effects).[40] For example, governance scholars at both international (Hale and Held, 2018) and domestic (Patterson et al., 2019) levels have identified the importance of constellations of causal mechanisms involved in bringing about substantive institutional changes in governance. Hence, ultimately the typology developed here opens up new opportunities for systematic, theory-driven comparative analysis to advance understanding of causal mechanisms involved in institutional remaking.

Pushing the focus on causality further reveals four conceptual clusters of explanatory variables (Figure 3). First, *political work* encompasses the activities of agents working for or against institutional changes, emphasizing the relevance of a wide variety of forms of agency in institutional remaking. Second, *contextual factors* encompass the active role of context in institutional remaking, not just as a backdrop but as generating causal force. Third, *slow-moving forces* encompass factors that may seem minor at any given moment, but which become causally significant over long timeframes. Fourth, *structural reconfiguration* encompasses the causal role of changes in system structure which progressively change the conditions for future activity over time. These clusters are not only interesting to observe in themselves, but, importantly, they also provide further ideas for generating hypotheses about causal processes and bridging between bodies of scholarship that focus on different but related phenomena.

Hence, the overall approach here helps to synthesize fragmented lines of thinking about how intentional institutional change can be conceptualized, explained, and accomplished. Moreover, it brings problem-driven thinking

---

[40] The interaction between uptake and dismantling is an immediate candidate. For example, in the context of European regulation, Jordan et al. (2013) identified that deregulation and re-regulation can involve complex interdependencies and mobilize differing political constituencies. Remaking regulation on climate change (i.e., deregulating while simultaneously re-regulating) is likely to be particularly unpredictable due to differing coalitions that mobilize for and against change.

Table 5 Decomposition of the five key areas of institutional production and their causal features

Category	Approaches	Causal features
Novelty	Endogenous creation of new elements	Political jostling; creation of ambiguity; politics of invention
	Changes in context triggering novelty	Shift in opportunity structures that afford challengers; action in response to instability
	Friction between institutional orders	Shift in opportunity structures that afford challengers; action in response to disjuncture
Uptake	Expansion of new elements	Outward, upward, or inward propagation; mobilization of coalitions for/against uptake
	Self-reinforcing feedback	Increasing durability of political/institutional trajectory over time
	Systemic effects	Nonlinear patterns of institutional development; flow-on consequences
Dismantling	Strategic dismantling	Political jostling; imposition of direction; mobilization of coalitions for/against removal
	Self-undermining feedback	Decreasing durability of political/institutional trajectory over time
	Abandonment	Shifts in attention; loss of authority/influence; politics of neglect
Stability	System persistence	Reinforcing activities; taken-for-grantedness; limited imagination of opportunity for change
	Active resistance	Political jostling; hostility to change; veto players
	Maintenance	Political jostling; conservative assertions; status quo behaviors
Interplay	Linkage/synergy	Outward view of boundaries; alignment seeking; cooperation
	Conflict/tension	Inward view of boundaries; power seeking; turf protection
	Co-development	Boundary transgression; complexity framing; ongoing adjustment

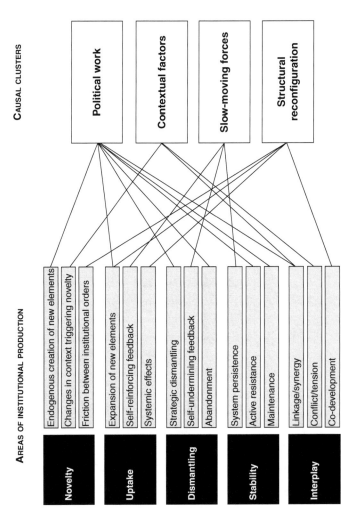

Figure 3 Relating the five areas of institutional production to broader causal clusters

from sustainability governance into dialogue with disciplinary traditions of thinking about institutional and political change, to develop a robust foundation on which the study of institutional remaking can be fruitfully advanced. This is significant because (interdisciplinary) sustainability governance scholarship often remains disconnected from (disciplinary) political science scholarship, which hinders a richer understanding of how multiplying institutional challenges faced in many domains, scales, and places can be tackled both in theory and practice. Indeed, the opportunity for productive dialogue among scholars enabled by the approach developed in this Element is one of its key overall contributions.

6 Advancing the Study of Institutional Remaking

The enquiry into institutional remaking conducted here leads to insights about processes of institutional change, concerning (i) the dichotomy between incremental and radical change, (ii) related and unrelated institutional development, and (iii) implications for navigating institutional trajectories that are "in-the-making." It contributes to broader institutional theory in several ways: (i) by providing a new way of apprehending action in institutional politics, (ii) by treating feasibility and desirability and endogenous properties, and (iii) by bringing institutional theory to bear on pressing real-world problems. It also leads to a novel research agenda to advance the study of institutional politics across a variety of issue areas.

6.1 Insights about Processes of Institutional Change

6.1.1 Beyond the Dichotomy of Incremental and Radical

Many scholars in sustainability governance draw a dichotomy between incremental and radical change.[41] For example, radical institutional change has been called for in regard to global environmental institutions (Biermann et al., 2012), climate change adaptation (Kates et al., 2012; Moser and Ekstrom, 2010; Wise et al., 2014), and climate change mitigation (IPCC, 2018, chapter 5). Here, "incremental" is frequently used in a pejorative way, referring to intentional action that is piecemeal, unambitious, and of limited consequence. While sometimes this is a useful critique, there is no inherent reason why incremental action cannot also be strategic, motivated by a transformative intent, and consequential. Hence, incremental action should not automatically be seen negatively, particularly when taking seriously the open-ended and developmental nature of institutional change. Along these lines, it has previously been suggested that the incremental/radical distinction is too stark (Patterson et al., 2017).

The typology presented here challenges the dichotomy of incremental versus radical institutional change, by showing why realizing intentional institutional change entails a multiplicity of complex political dynamics that probably require sustained change over long timeframes. Sweeping reforms may not often be possible given that moves to introduce changes inevitably generate counter-reactions, are unavoidably encumbered by history, and must mesh with a particular context (e.g., culture, practices, materiality). Yet, at the same time, the approach developed here demonstrates the many ways in which institutions

---

[41] Scale, timeframe, and normative criteria matter when judging whether something is radical or not, and to whom. For example, an intervention that seems radical at a particular scale (e.g., such as a difficult regulatory reform within a national government) may seem incremental at another scale (e.g., to a community concerned with immediate climate action).

are also dynamic, which suggests that opportunities for remaking institutions may be present on a relatively ongoing basis. Hence, what matters is understanding how and where opportunities for change lie, how changes may be realized, and the ways in which efforts to bring about intentional changes are conditioned by existing setups.[42] Attempts to bring about radical changes must be analyzed carefully as provisional and unfolding, full of unintended and unpredictable effects, and subject to constant challenge, rather than simply assumed to be once-off moves that either succeed or fail.

More deeply, the approach developed here calls into question assumptions of institutional equilibria, which often underlie views of both incremental change (as failing to depart from an established equilibria) and radical change (as supposedly bringing about a new equilibria). Institutional scholars have long pointed out that such equilibria are overly simplistic, as institutions are subject to constant friction (Orren and Skowronek, 1996), political struggle (Mahoney and Thelen, 2010), ideational challenge (Lieberman, 2002), and slow-moving shifts (Pierson, 2004). Hence settlements are at best temporary and ultimately political rather than functional. However, sustainability scholars still often seem to implicitly – and even explicitly[43] – invoke equilibria in explanations of institutional change. This is done, for example, through defining normative goals for sustainability transformations, which assume a new equilibrium to be reached, which is defined ex ante. Conversely, the approach developed here emphasizes the provisional and unfolding character of institutional remaking, treating outcomes as an empirical question, and emphasizing the underlying political dynamics which produce any particular institutional trajectory.

6.1.2 Related and Unrelated Institutional Development

The typology developed here shows why institutional remaking cannot be seen as occurring on a blank slate but is encumbered by the effects of past decisions, entangled with heterogeneous social contexts and material linkages, and conditioned by political relations and discourses. Moreover, any given institutional arena

---

[42] Oberthür (2016) makes a somewhat similar argument in the context of enhancing interplay between international regimes, when arguing that "[a]dvances can and have to be made on the basis of the existing ... structures that can be developed gradually and incrementally" (p. 89), which is also a "positive message" because building on existing structures means that "[w]e thus do not need to wait for major reform before we can start making progress" (p. 102).

[43] For example, a large body of literature on the governance of "social-ecological systems" is premised on the presence of equilibria, which provide attractors for stable system states, where radical change involves moving from one stable state equilibria to another (e.g., Otto et al., 2020; Westley et al., 2011). This idea also underlies the large body of work on sustainability transitions, which explores how socio-technical systems may transition from one stable state to another (more desirable) one.

(viewed as a set of rules that structure a particular decision-making arena) will be connected to many other rules and arenas. Consequently, "once institutions are in place, they facilitate the adoption of other, complementary institutions" (Pierson, 2004, p. 150). This would suggest that institutional remaking is most likely to occur in directions that are *related* to what came before, rather than as a radical break in an *unrelated* direction. On the other hand, the urgency of climate change and other major challenges, as well as increasing institutional breakdown, appears to increasingly demand radical interventions and, therefore, unrelated institutional development (Section 1). The typology developed here does not preclude radical institutional change, but it does draw attention to the complex political dynamics likely to be associated with it. For example, the typology makes clear why a focus on radical novelty alone is not sufficient, but we must also pay attention to other key political dynamics (e.g., How and why does uptake of novelty occur? What must be dismantled to allow uptake, and how does this occur? What forms of stability work against change? Do other linked arenas support or hinder new changes?).

The need to move from simplistic calls for radical change to much more nuanced analysis of the complex political dynamics involved chimes with observations of some sustainability scholars, who soberly observe that a concern for radical change can actually focus too much attention on prescription of (future) goals rather than an understanding of opportunities for change in the present. For example, Dryzek (2016, 951) suggests that "it is more productive to start from where we are now and think in terms of the dynamics of institutional change and available opportunities for overcoming problematic path dependency . . . [which] in turn requires context-sensitive empirical analysis and evaluation of existing institutions and practices before thinking about prescription." Similarly, Newell (2015, p. 72) argues in regard to the political economy of green transformations that "the longer term goal . . . has to be a transformation of capitalism rather than a transformation within, but we have to start the analysis on the terrain of the here and now and the actually existing political economy, as it is, not as we would like it to be." The next logical step would be to focus on *the ways in which social action is produced in the present* and contributes to unfolding patterns of institutional development, which is the starting point for the approach in this Element. Moreover, the approach developed here also provides a comprehensive frame for evaluating institutional remaking in processual terms, by focusing on comparative improvement, directionality of institutional change, and capacity for social action (Section 4). This opens up opportunities to examine the potential for radical change while remaining grounded in the reality of imperfect starting points and anchored in the present rather than a speculative future. Yet, at the same time, it pushes analysis to focus on institutional changes that are emerging, or have potential to emerge, rather than only looking backward to past changes.

6.1.3 Navigating Institutional Trajectories In-the-Making

Social action to remake institutions can perhaps most aptly be seen as navigational, given the multiplicity of political dynamics and the provisional and unfolding character of institutional change. Institutions are neither entirely fluid nor entirely ossified. Institutional remaking may lead to changes and reconfigurations, which are nonetheless partial and incomplete and subject to political challenge. For example, Stripple and Bulkeley (2019, p. 53) argue that, in the context of decarbonization, pathways of change are cultivated through "a logic and practice of wayfinding that is pursued with the intention of realising a response to climate change but . . . always bound up with other entities, goals and interests." Institutional remaking thus requires ongoing effort and adjustment to shape institutional trajectories.

Yet institutional remaking is not just about individual activities, but also coordination. A key challenge is to understand how coordination can be accomplished to realize institutional changes, which may be at most provisional, yet still require action in many ways simultaneously to succeed. While there are long-standing currents of skepticism about the merits of intentional intervention and coordination in public governance (e.g., Hayek, 1991; Rittel and Webber, 1973), institutional scholars from various angles have tried to find ways to reconcile intentionality and spontaneity (e.g., Kingston and Caballero, 2009; North, 2010; Young, 2013). The typology developed in this Element, identifying several key areas of institutional production within attempts to (intentionally) remake institutions, helps to disaggregate the various forces pulling in different directions and thereby provides new ways to interrogate coordination or its absence.

Altogether, this challenges scholars to move from seeing institutional remaking as a stepwise activity (whether incremental or radical) to one that is better characterized by a branching or even rhizomatic pattern. Future institutional trajectories are inherently connected to complex historical patterns and contexts and therefore have limited degrees of freedom from one moment to the next, but over time they may nonetheless develop in unpredictable – and potentially transformative – ways. Under this view, "positive" incremental action (i.e., action that is strategic and motivated by a transformative intent) may be most associated with *related* institutional development where new trajectories emerge gradually,[44] whereas "radical" action may be most associated with *unrelated* institutional development where new trajectories emerge more abruptly. But in all cases, institutional change is inevitably wedded to prior structurings that cannot be simply cleaved from one moment to another. Viewing institutional remaking as

---

[44] Contrasted against "negative" incremental action (i.e., piecemeal and unambitious action), which is insufficient to move beyond path dependencies.

a navigational endeavor, leading to branching or rhizomatic development, thus reflects an inseparable connection to the past, while also permitting continuous development in the future. Yet it also invites probing of possibilities, what may be thought of as the potentiality of a given moment, which emerges through actual social action.

6.2 Contributions to Broader Institutional Theory

6.2.1 Apprehending Action in Institutional Politics

Institutional remaking centers on examining the nature of contested action within institutional arenas – the institutional politics of intervention. This is distinguished from typical approaches to institutional design, where design is treated as an independent variable for explaining institutional change, but itself largely remains a black box[45] (Section 3.4). From another angle, it is now commonplace (although not entirely new)[46] for scholars to recommend experimentation as a way of thinking about societal improvement in an uncertain world, a strategy that resonates closely with the logic of navigational thinking (Section 6.1.3). For example, experimentation appears to be a normative implication of polycentric governance theory (Jordan et al., 2018), and empirically experimentation has been observed in practice within transnational and subnational arenas of climate change governance (Castán Broto and Bulkeley, 2013; Hoffmann, 2011). Dryzek (2016) also alludes to experimentation as a way of cultivating institutional reflexivity under the profoundly changing circumstances of the Anthropocene. However, this tends to focus on a particular aspect of social action (which locates as a form of "Novelty" in the typology developed here) and often does not look much at consequences for institutional politics over time. Instead, the approach developed here focuses on the production of social action in a wider range of (interconnected) ways, recognizing the weight of the past, while oriented toward understanding how institutional changes may be intentionally pursued.

6.2.2 Endogenizing Feasibility and Desirability

An enduring challenge of studying institutional intervention is the question of how to treat normative goals, given that any intervention will inevitably be contested. Hence, there may almost never be consensus about how, and indeed even whether, institutions should be remade within a given arena. In the context

---

[45] Notwithstanding exceptions seeking a processual (Barzelay and Gallego, 2006) and design-oriented (Barzelay and Thompson, 2007) understanding of policy reform.

[46] For example, the American pragmatist philosopher John Dewey suggested the need for experimentation in societal problem-solving at the beginning of the twentieth century.

of calls for rapid climate action, scholars have recently been giving increased attention to the political feasibility of interventions (e.g., Andersen, 2019; Dryzek et al., 2019; Patterson et al., 2018; Pralle, 2009), reflecting a concern for support and practicality of political action. When considering any particular institutional intervention, it is important for analysis not to simply impose an outsider-defined view of desirability and feasibility. In other words, these attributes cannot be assessed externally to context. Consequently, this requires an interpretive approach to view institutional remaking with reference to endogenously defined norms and goals held by certain actors within an institutional arena (which may itself be nested within broader arenas and therefore norms and goals). This approach endogenizes feasibility and desirability by examining activities and contestations in situ, seeking to understand how dilemmas are perceived by involved actors, and the consequences for institutional development. The heuristic typology proposed here (Section 5) reflects this, since it needs to be anchored by a particular issue and stance toward social improvement, as reflected by the actors attempting to remake certain institutions.

This has implications for how institutional remaking can be observed and evaluated: If institutional remaking is viewed with reference to endogenous norms and goals, then how can we judge overall performance when studying any given case? An increasingly common approach in sustainability literature for understanding trajectories of change in governance over time is the notion of "pathways" (e.g., Rosenbloom, 2017; Wise et al., 2014). Yet, while this is valuable in encouraging a broad perspective in evaluation (both temporally and systemically), it often strays toward implying a singular trajectory, which is outsider-defined ex ante. Moreover, it risks responding to the uncertainty of the future by reintroducing a sense of managerialism, implying mappable order and even prescriptive influence over future patterns of change. Instead, the approach to evaluation developed here (Section 4) draws on notions of comparative improvement, directionality, and the ongoing capacity for social action as a way to more open-endedly explore institutional development, which allows for both intentional and non-intentional causes. This does not predefine trajectories of institutional development, but at the same time, it scrutinizes the extent to which such trajectories meet key needs of societies, particularly related to sustainability and social equity.

The evaluation frame avoids the assumption that a transcendental norm is needed to orient social action (following Sen 2009). Different actors may be motivated by different and even competing norms, yet what matters in analyzing institutional remaking is the social action that ultimately arises and its (institutional) consequences. Yet this leaves unanswered puzzling questions about how to judge the extent to which emergent institutional trajectories actually do address sustainability and social equity issues, such as the urgent need for climate action. How can this be reconciled?

In essence, the evaluation proposed separates institutional development outcomes from normative goals for social improvement, rather than conflating them. Sustainability scholars commonly conflate institutional outcomes and normative goals for social improvement, whereas political scientists commonly only consider institutional outcomes but not normative goals. Sen (2009) proposes that normative goals for social improvement can only ever be arrived at through democratic social choice, which may then motivate comparative improvements made by societies over time (in lieu of transcendent normative goals). But on the other hand, the need for rapid, large-scale, and crosscutting climate action as understood scientifically to be required (Section 1) challenges this line of thinking on the basis of urgency and "objective" problem pressure. When studying institutional remaking, the focus turns to understanding which normative goals matter within a given arena and whether and when to pay attention to normative goals that lie outside of the particular arena in evaluation. For example, if a political community does not give much attention to climate change, could an analysis still consider wider normative goals, such as the views of other societies, or based on what is known scientifically about climate impacts on that community? Would this be imposing an exogenous normative goal, thus essentially replicating a transcendental logic?

Following the approach of Sen (2009), this could be approached through employing the conceptual device of the "impartial spectator," which permits critique from voices "outside" the immediate unit of analysis as valid form of contestation. More practically, analysis could proceed by considering (i) whether there are in fact (potentially marginalized) endogenous views around the issue at stake (e.g., climate change), which might indeed be sources of social action; (ii) whether a larger arena should be considered in analysis on the basis of plausible causal relations, and which encompasses a wider range of views and political actors, and thus potential for institutional dynamism; or (iii) if none or very few actors are concerned with the issue at stake, then perhaps there is simply no case for studying institutional remaking in that arena at that particular time – it may be a case of severe path dependency or stagnation. But it is also important to note that the approach developed in this Element would suggest that there may almost always be reasons to expect some degree of institutional dynamism, given that both endogenous and exogenous circumstances are always dynamic, and even institutional stability can be seen as a property which is not self-evident but must be constantly produced and reproduced (Beunen et al., 2017). As Orren and Skowreneck (1996, p. 140) point out: "Once it is appreciated that political settings do not typically present a single set of institutional constraints, the potential for creativity by actors of all sorts becomes evident."

6.2.3 Putting Institutional Theory to Work

The overall argument in this Element started out by emphasizing the need for an approach that helps to find solutions to institutional weaknesses and failures, especially in a prospective way that goes beyond explanations of past events only, and also gives insight into how to tackle future problems (Section 1.6). In response, the approach developed here is rooted in understanding the production of social action in institutional settings, while also recognizing linkages with wider contextual factors such as heterogeneity, materiality, and environmental change. It focuses on understanding processes that are unfolding and in-the-making in the contemporary world, with outcomes that are partial and provisional, but nonetheless judgeable through viewing them as part of an unfolding trajectory of institutional development (Section 4).

This opens up an innovative new way of studying intentional institutional change, which is distinct from both input-oriented approaches (e.g., design, capacity) and output-oriented approaches (e.g., performance), by unravelling generalizable areas of institutional production which are constitutive of intentional institutional change. This contributes to enabling process-oriented explanation and theorizing of institutional change by providing an analytical foundation for the generation and testing of hypotheses. This approach can thereby support systematic comparative analysis across places, and potentially also domains (e.g., climate change, sustainability, and beyond), which thus moves definitively beyond "comparative statics" (following Dryzek, 2016, p. 943) in analyzing institutional change. This is significant because scholars are increasingly concerned with tackling institutional shortcomings and failures, especially under climate change (Cosens et al., 2014; Craig, 2010; Dryzek, 2016; Wenta et al., 2018). However, we largely lack the analytical tools to understand how problems may be addressed without waiting for manifest failure to occur. Doing so demands that scholars move beyond purely ex post or ex ante approaches to embrace unfolding activities and changes in the present, that is, those that are *in-the-making*.

Ultimately, the approach developed here advances a research agenda that brings theoretical institutional insights to bear on addressing real-world problems, while also opening up new opportunities to enrich institutional theory with empirical insights stemming from contemporary efforts to address multiplying institutional weaknesses and failures in political life. It also invigorates institutional change scholarship by bringing in consideration of directionality and ends, which are often noticeably absent. On the other hand, it enriches sustainability scholarship with insights from rich traditions of thinking about institutional change, which remain underutilized on the whole. As such, the approach straddles between positive analysis ("what is") and normative analysis ("what ought to be") through an interpretive political disposition. It also opens the door to considering the "potentiality" of what *could be*, through a focus on the production of social action, and resulting institutional trajectories. This notion of potentiality is an intriguing line of thinking for future work.

7 Conclusions

This Element set out to explore how we can address a growing number of situations of institutional weakness and failure in domestic politics, particularly in light of the urgent need for ambitious action, and even societal transformations, on climate change. The departure point is the need to understand how it may be possible to *remake* political institutions, both in anticipation of, and in response to, climate change, while also recognizing that such action is unavoidably embedded within complex and nonideal existing institutional settings. Climate change is both a crucial substantive area for institutional remaking, as well as a salient case study of the extent to which domestic political institutions are capable of proactively responding to profoundly shifting circumstances confronting societies across the world in the twenty-first century.

In addressing this challenge, this Element makes several original contributions. First, it advances a new argument about the need to remake political institutions across a variety of issue areas. Second, it develops an analytical foundation for studying institutional remaking, including an observation/evaluation frame, and a heuristic typology that disaggregates multiple areas of institutional production involved in attempts to remake institutions, thereby providing a structured set of "entry points" for analysis. Third, it brings sustainability scholarship into closer dialogue with scholarship on processes of institutional change and development. Fourth, it makes possible analysis of provisional and unfolding processes in institutional politics, which can otherwise be difficult to apprehend. Fifth, it elucidates a variety of insights about how institutional change is conceptualized in sustainability and conversely contributes insights to broader institutional theory from sustainability. Altogether, this opens up a new research agenda on the politics of responding proactively to institutional breakdown.

7.1 Research Agenda

Sustainability scholars concerned with understanding governance in the domestic political sphere increasingly find useful insights in institutional theory. For example, recent work considers climate policy (Jordan and Matt, 2014), low-carbon transitions (e.g., Andrews-Speed, 2016; Lockwood et al., 2017; Roberts et al., 2018; Roberts and Geels, 2019), and climate change adaptation (e.g., Patterson et al., 2019; Patterson and Huitema, 2019) through a developmental institutional lens. This work collectively illuminates understudied institutional dimensions of sustainability transformations, since institutions are not often studied directly in this scholarship. Yet the current state of thinking about the role of institutions in sustainability transformations remains underdeveloped and does not provide a clear foundation for conceptualizing exactly how political institutions (often viewed as sluggish or even recalcitrant) may change. Such a foundation is exactly what this Element provides, with the ultimate hope that we can move toward better understanding of how institutions may be developed in directions that help to address major societal problems.

On the basis of the enquiry undertaken here, a variety of important new directions for future work arise, from both analytical and strategic angles (Table 6). Analytical questions provide the opportunity to strengthen our explanations of institutional change and development on pressing contemporary issues. Strategic questions provide the opportunity to find new approaches for intervention toward transformations in governance. Altogether, these questions provide a novel way of thinking about pressing new challenges arising in contemporary governance, as well as several long-standing theoretical and practical issues. They thus provide a roadmap for path-breaking research likely to yield new ways of understanding institutional matters of interest to analysts and practitioners alike.

Advancing an agenda on institutional remaking requires – and readily invites – comparative work across diverse settings. Institutional settings are almost infinitely complex and diverse (Ostrom 2005), which means that the typology developed here is only a first step toward getting a better handle on how institutional improvement may be realized in many different areas of political life. For example, comparative work (only considering the domestic political sphere) could be delineated on the basis of places (both within and across countries), political systems (e.g., presidential or parliamentary, federal or unitary), levels of order (e.g., city, state/province, national), and issue areas (e.g., climate change, sustainability, welfare, economy, migration), among others.

While this Element is motivated by a concern for addressing institutional weaknesses and failures on public good issues (such as climate change, sustainability, and social equity), the approach developed here also potentially has a more generalizable quality. Conceivably, attempts to remake institutions toward a range of political agendas witnessed in contemporary politics (e.g., globalization, neoliberalization) could also be studied through the same basic approach. Yet this would certainly require modification of what is meant by "social improvement" to carefully specify whose agenda was the anchor for analysis. This would enable an even wider universe of potential cases through which to study and scrutinize the remaking of institutions within domestic politics.

7.2 Final Remarks

In a changing world, institutional success may be marked more by the ability of institutions and governance systems to adapt to and anticipate change, rather than by success in regulating or optimizing access to resources per se (following

Table 6 Key research questions for future work on institutional remaking

Angle	Research questions
Analytical	Which specific *causal mechanisms* operate within each area of institutional production (both individually and combinatorially), and under which *conditions*?
	What is the *diversity of forms* of institutional remaking across institutional arenas and over time? Are there any *patterns* that can be discerned (e.g., across places, types of political systems, levels of institutional order, or issue areas)?
	How can we reliably recognize the formation of *(new) institutional trajectories* and their *directionality*, especially at a nascent or ambiguous stage?
	How do changes in the *wider ideational context* (e.g., imaginaries of the future, protest and mobilization) influence attempts to remake institutions?
Strategic	Where do *possibilities* lie for "incremental change with a strategic agenda" in a given setting? How might they be *targeted*, both individually and in combination? How might changes in different/disparate areas be *"joined-up"* to support cumulation and, ultimately, transformation in governance?
	How can we identify institutional changes that are *emerging*, or have *potential* to emerge? How do related and unrelated institutional developments interact to *redirect* an institutional trajectory over time (e.g., complementary, antagonistic, or idiosyncratic effects)?
	How can *coordination* can be accomplished toward institutional renewal (e.g., considering both intentionality and spontaneity), given that institutional changes may be at most provisional and without clear end point, yet still require action in multiple simultaneous ways to succeed?

Dryzek, 2016). But the challenge, then, is how to get there, beginning from the imperfect starting point of the present – in other words, *how to remake institutions in situ*. Paradoxically, when we talk about societal transformations for climate change, we should not lose sight of the fact that in some ways it is an unprecedented challenge in human history, while at the same time, also an extension of ongoing and often mundane institutional politics.

The focus on climate change governance, including efforts to realize societal transformations, highlights the central role of institutional politics, which is still surprisingly understudied in sustainability governance scholarship. The focus on the domestic political sphere is also significant, given the "need for more nuanced, and regionally and nationally specific theories of change ... [which] requires the building of national strategies and locating transformations within understandings of national political dynamics" (Scoones et al., 2015, p. 21). Yet the implications of the argument also extend far beyond climate change. For example, Aligica (2014, p. 204) observes that "self-governing, democratic systems are always fragile enterprises. Future citizens need to understand that they participate in the constitution and reconstitution of rule-governed polities." Yet it is not just future citizens who are confronted with the need to reconstitute rule-governed polities, but also, unavoidably, those in the present. Creating the tools, frameworks, and insights to help do so is an immensely important task, which scholars are compelled to help tackle. It is not an understatement to say that political performance and societal well-being now depend, more than ever, on our ability to remake political institutions.

References

Abbott, K. W., 2012. The transnational regime complex for climate change. *Environment and Planning C: Government and Policy* 30, 571–590. https://doi.org/10.1068/c11127

Abson, D. J., Fischer, J., Leventon, J., Newig, J., Schomerus, T., Vilsmaier, U., von Wehrden, H., Abernethy, P., Ives, C. D., Jager, N. W., Lang, D. J., 2017. Leverage points for sustainability transformation. *Ambio* 46, 30–39. https://doi.org/10.1007/s13280-016–0800-y

Aligica, P. D., 2014. *Institutional Diversity and Political Economy: The Ostroms and Beyond.* Oxford University Press, Oxford; New York.

Andersen, M. S., 2019. The politics of carbon taxation: How varieties of policy style matter. *Environmental Politics* 28, 1084–1104. https://doi.org/10.1080/09644016.2019.1625134

Andrews-Speed, P., 2016. Applying institutional theory to the low-carbon energy transition. *Energy Research & Social Science* 13, 216–225. https://doi.org/10.1016/j.erss.2015.12.011

Anguelovski, I., Carmin, J., 2011. Something borrowed, everything new: Innovation and institutionalization in urban climate governance. *Current Opinion in Environmental Sustainability* 3, 169–175. https://doi.org/10.1016/j.cosust.2010.12.017

Aylett, A., 2015. Institutionalizing the urban governance of climate change adaptation: Results of an international survey. *Urban Climate* 14, 4–16. https://doi.org/10.1016/j.uclim.2015.06.005

Aylett, A., 2013. The socio-institutional dynamics of urban climate governance: A comparative analysis of innovation and change in Durban (KZN, South Africa) and Portland (OR, USA). *Urban Studies* 50, 1386–1402. https://doi.org/10.1177/0042098013480968

Barzelay, M., Gallego, R., 2006. From "new institutionalism" to "institutional processualism": Advancing knowledge about public management policy change. *Governance: An International Journal of Policy, Administration, and Institutions* 19, 531–557. https://doi.org/10.1111/j.1468-0491.2006.00339.x

Barzelay, M., Thompson, F., April 3, 2007. Making Public Management a Design-Oriented Science. Available at SSRN: https://ssrn.com/abstract=979041 or http://dx.doi.org/10.2139/ssrn.979041

Baumgartner, F. R., Jones, B. D., 2009. *Agendas and Instability in American Politics*, 2nd ed., Chicago Studies in American Politics. University of Chicago Press, Chicago, IL.

Beetham, D., 2013. *The Legitimation of Power*, 2nd ed., Political Analysis. Palgrave Macmillan, Houndmills, Basingstoke, Hampshire; New York, NY.

Berchin, I. I., Valduga, I. B., Garcia, J., de Andrade Guerra, J. B. S. O., 2017. Climate change and forced migrations: An effort towards recognizing climate refugees. *Geoforum* 84, 147–150. https://doi.org/10.1016/j.geoforum.2017.06.022

Bernstein, S., Hoffmann, M., 2019. Climate politics, metaphors and the fractal carbon trap. *Nature Climate Change* 9, 919–925. https://doi.org/10.1038/s41558-019-0618-2

Bernstein, S., Hoffmann, M., 2018a. Decarbonisation: The politics of transformation, in: Jordan, A., Huitema, D., van Asselt, H., Forster, J. (Eds.), *Governing Climate Change*. Cambridge University Press, Cambridge, United Kingdom. pp. 248–265. https://doi.org/10.1017/9781108284646.015

Bernstein, S., Hoffmann, M., 2018b. The politics of decarbonization and the catalytic impact of subnational climate experiments. *Policy Sciences* 51, 189–211. https://doi.org/10.1007/s11077-018-9314-8

Betsill, M., Dubash, N. K., Paterson, M., van Asselt, H., Vihma, A., Winkler, H., 2015. Building productive links between the UNFCCC and the broader global climate governance landscape. *Global Environmental Politics* 15, 1–10. https://doi.org/10.1162/GLEP_a_00294

Betsill, M. M., Benney, T. M., Gerlak, A. K. (Eds.), 2020. *Agency in Earth System Governance*, 1st ed., Cambridge University Press, Cambridge, United Kingdom. https://doi.org/10.1017/9781108688277

Beunen, R., Patterson, J., Van Assche, K., 2017. Governing for resilience: The role of institutional work. *Current Opinion in Environmental Sustainability* 28, 10–16. https://doi.org/10.1016/j.cosust.2017.04.010

Beunen, R., Patterson, J. J., 2019. Analysing institutional change in environmental governance: Exploring the concept of "institutional work." *Journal of Environmental Planning and Management* 62, 12–29. https://doi.org/10.1080/09640568.2016.1257423

Biagini, B., Bierbaum, R., Stults, M., Dobardzic, S., McNeeley, S. M., 2014. A typology of adaptation actions: A global look at climate adaptation actions financed through the Global Environment Facility. *Global Environmental Change* 25, 97–108. https://doi.org/10.1016/j.gloenvcha.2014.01.003

Biermann, F., Abbott, K., Andresen, S., Bäckstrand, K., Bernstein, S., Betsill, M. M., Bulkeley, H., Cashore, B., Clapp, J., Folke, C., others, 2012. Navigating the Anthropocene: Improving earth system governance. *Science* 335, 1306–1307.

Biermann, F., Pattberg, P., van Asselt, H., Zelli, F., 2009. The fragmentation of global governance architectures: A framework for analysis. *Global Environmental Politics* 9, 14–40. https://doi.org/10.1162/glep.2009.9.4.14

Birkland, T. A., 1998. Focusing events, mobilization, and agenda setting. *Journal of Public Policy* 18, 53–74.

Blome, K., Fischer-Lescano, A., Franzki, H., Markard, N., Oeter, S. (Eds.), 2016. *Contested Regime Collisions: Norm Fragmentation in World Society.* Cambridge University Press, Cambridge. https://doi.org/10.1017/CBO978131 6411230

Bloom, D. E., 2019. For the economy to cope with an ageing population, we must identify new solutions – here's how [WWW Document]. World Economic Forum Agenda. URL www.weforum.org/agenda/2019/10/age ing-economics-population-health/

Boin, A., 2005. *The Politics of Crisis Management Public Leadership under Pressure.* Cambridge University Press, Cambridge, UK; New York, NY.

Bregman, R., 2018. *Utopia for Realists*, Paperback ed., Bloomsbury, London.

Brisbois, M. C., 2019. Powershifts: A framework for assessing the growing impact of decentralized ownership of energy transitions on political decision-making. *Energy Research & Social Science* 50, 151–161. https://doi.org/10.1016/j.erss.2018.12.003

Brouwer, S., Huitema, D., 2018. Policy entrepreneurs and strategies for change. *Regional Environmental Change* 18, 1259–1272. https://doi.org/10.1007/s10113-017-1139-z

Brown, J., Granoff, I., 2018. Deep decarbonization by 2050: Rethinking the role of climate finance. Climate Policy Initiative, and Climate Works Foundation. www.climatepolicyinitiative.org/wp-content/uploads/2018/07/Deep-decar bonization-by-2050-rethinking-the-role-of-climate-finance.pdf

Brown, K., Adger, W. N., Cinner, J. E., 2019. Moving climate change beyond the tragedy of the commons. *Global Environmental Change* 54, 61–63. https://doi.org/10.1016/j.gloenvcha.2018.11.009

Brown, R. R., Farrelly, M. A., Loorbach, D. A., 2013. Actors working the institutions in sustainability transitions: The case of Melbourne's stormwater management. *Global Environmental Change* 23, 701–718. https://doi.org/10.1016/j.gloenvcha.2013.02.013

Buchan, D., 2012. *The Energiewende – Germany's Gamble* (No. SP 26). Oxford Institute for Energy Studies, Oxford, UK.

Bulkeley, H., Andonova, L. B., Betsill, M. M., Compagnon, D., Hale, T., Hoffman, M. J., Newell, P., Paterson, M., Roger, C., Vandeveer, S. D., 2014. *Transnational Climate Change Governance.* Cambridge University Press, New York, NY.

Bulkeley, H., Castán Broto, V., 2013. Government by experiment? Global cities and the governing of climate change. *Transactions of the Institute of British Geographers* 38, 361–375.

Bulkeley, H., Paterson, M., Stripple, J. (Eds.), 2016. *Towards a Cultural Politics of Climate Change: Devices, Desires and Dissent.* Cambridge University Press, Cambridge. https://doi.org/10.1017/CBO9781316694473

Burch, S., Gupta, A., Inoue, C. Y. A., Kalfagianni, A., Persson, Å. , Gerlak, A. K., Ishii, A., Patterson, J., Pickering, J., Scobie, M., Van der Heijden, J., Vervoort, J., Adler, C., Bloomfield, M., Djalante, R., Dryzek, J., Galaz, V., Gordon, C., Harmon, R., Jinnah, S., Kim, R. E., Olsson, L., Van Leeuwen, J., Ramasar, V., Wapner, P., Zondervan, R., 2019. New directions in earth system governance research. Earth System Governance 100006. https://doi.org/10.1016/j.esg.2019.100006

Busby, J., 2019. Climate change as anarchy: The need for a new structural theory of IR. Duck of Minerva. URL https://duckofminerva.com/2019/04/climate-change-as-anarchy-the-need-for-a-new-structural theory-of-ir.html

Busby, J., 2018. Warming world: Why climate change matters more than anything else. *Foreign Affairs* 97(4), 49–55.

Capoccia, G., 2016. When do institutions "bite"? Historical institutionalism and the politics of institutional change. *Comparative Political Studies* 49, 1095–1127. https://doi.org/10.1177/0010414015626449

Carmin, J., Anguelovski, I., Roberts, D., 2012. Urban climate adaptation in the global south: Planning in an emerging policy domain. *Journal of Planning Education and Research* 32, 18–32. https://doi.org/10.1177/0739456X11430951

Carter, J. G., Cavan, G., Connelly, A., Guy, S., Handley, J., Kazmierczak, A., 2015. Climate change and the city: Building capacity for urban adaptation. *Progress in Planning* 95, 1–66. https://doi.org/10.1016/j.progress.2013.08.001

Cash, D. W., Clark, W. C., Alcock, F., Dickson, N. M., Eckley, N., Guston, D. H., Jäger, J., Mitchell, R. B., 2003. Knowledge systems for sustainable development. *Proceedings of the National Academy of Sciences* 100, 8086–8091.

Castán Broto, V., Bulkeley, H., 2013. A survey of urban climate change experiments in 100 cities. *Global Environmental Change* 23, 92–102. https://doi.org/10.1016/j.gloenvcha.2012.07.005

Chan, S., van Asselt, H., Hale, T., Abbott, K. W., Beisheim, M., Hoffmann, M., Guy, B., Höhne, N., Hsu, A., Pattberg, P., Pauw, P., Ramstein, C., Widerberg, O., 2015. Reinvigorating international climate policy: A comprehensive framework for effective nonstate action. *Global Policy* 6, 466–473. https://doi.org/10.1111/1758-5899.12294

Chapron, G., Epstein, Y., Trouwborst, A., López-Bao, J. V., 2017. Bolster legal boundaries to stay within planetary boundaries. *Nature Ecology & Evolution* 1, 0086. https://doi.org/10.1038/s41559-017-0086

Conference of the Parties, 2015. Paris Agreement. *United Nations Framework Convention on Climate Change* 12, December 2015.

Cook, S. D. N., Wagenaar, H., 2012. Navigating the eternally unfolding present: Toward an epistemology of practice. *The American Review of Public Administration* 42, 3–38. https://doi.org/10.1177/0275074011407404

Cosens, B. A., Gunderson, L., Chaffin, B. C., November 4, 2014. *The Adaptive Water Governance Project: Assessing Law, Resilience and Governance in Regional Socio-Ecological Water Systems Facing a Changing Climate* 51 Idaho Law Review 1, Available at SSRN: https://ssrn.com/abstract=2519236 .

Craig, R. K., 2010. "Stationarity is dead" – Long live transformation: Five principles for climate change adaptation law. *Harvard Environmental Law Review* 34, 9–73.

de Mooij, R., 2006. *Reinventing the Welfare State (No. 60)*. CPB Netherlands Bureau for Economic Policy Analysis, The Hague, The Netherlands.

Devlin, C., Hendrix, C. S., 2014. Trends and triggers redux: Climate change, rainfall, and interstate conflict. *Political Geography* 43, 27–39. https://doi.org/10.1016/j.polgeo.2014.07.001

DiMaggio, P. J., Powell, W. W., 1983. The iron cage revisited: Institutional isomorphism and collective rationality in organizational fields. *American Sociological Review* 48, 147. https://doi.org/10.2307/2095101

Dryzek, J. S., 2016. Institutions for the Anthropocene: Governance in a changing earth system. *British Journal of Political Science* 46, 937–956. https://doi.org/10.1017/S0007123414000453

Dryzek, J. S., Bowman, Q., Kuyper, J., Pickering, J., Sass, J., Stevenson, H., 2019. *Deliberative Global Governance*, 1st ed., Cambridge University Press, Cambridge, United Kingdom. https://doi.org/10.1017/9781108762922

Eakin, H., Lemos, M. C., 2010. Institutions and change: The challenge of building adaptive capacity in Latin America. *Global Environmental Change* 20, 1–3. https://doi.org/10.1016/j.gloenvcha.2009.08.002

Ericksen, P. J., Ingram, J. S. I., Liverman, D. M., 2009. Food security and global environmental change: Emerging challenges. *Environmental Science & Policy* 12, 373–377. https://doi.org/10.1016/j.envsci.2009.04.007

Ethington, P. J., McDaniel, J. A., 2007. Political places and institutional spaces: The intersection of political science and political geography. *Annual Review of Political Science* 10, 127–142. https://doi.org/10.1146/annurev.polisci.10.080505.100522

European Commission, 2019. Communication from the Commission to the European Parliament, The European Council, The Council, The European Economic and Social Committee and the Committee of the Regions: The European Green Deal (No. 11. 12.2019 COM(2019) 640 final). European

Commission, Brussels. https://eur-lex.europa.eu/legal-content/EN/TXT/?uri=COM:2019:640:FIN

Falkner, R., 2016. The Paris agreement and the new logic of international climate politics. *International Affairs* 92, 1107–1125. https://doi.org/10.1111/1468-2346.12708

Falleti, T. G., Lynch, J. F., 2009. Context and causal mechanisms in political analysis. *Comparative Political Studies* 42, 1143–1166. https://doi.org/10.1177/0010414009331724

Farrelly, M., Brown, R., 2011. Rethinking urban water management: Experimentation as a way forward? *Global Environmental Change* 21, 721–732.

Fazey, I., Moug, P., Allen, S., Beckmann, K., Blackwood, D., Bonaventura, M., Burnett, K., Danson, M., Falconer, R., Gagnon, A. S., Harkness, R., Hodgson, A., Holm, L., Irvine, K. N., Low, R., Lyon, C., Moss, A., Moran, C., Naylor, L., O'Brien, K., Russell, S., Skerratt, S., Rao-Williams, J., Wolstenholme, R., 2018. Transformation in a changing climate: A research agenda. *Climate and Development* 10, 197–217. https://doi.org/10.1080/17565529.2017.1301864

Feola, G., Geoghegan, H., Arnall, A., 2019. *Climate and Culture: Multidisciplinary Perspectives on a Warming World*. Cambridge University Press, Cambridge, UK.

Frantzeskaki, N., Kabisch, N., McPhearson, T., 2016. Advancing urban environmental governance: Understanding theories, practices and processes shaping urban sustainability and resilience. *Environmental Science & Policy* 62, 1–6. https://doi.org/10.1016/j.envsci.2016.05.008

Freudenberger, M., Miller, D., 2010. *USAID Issue Brief: Climate Change, Property Rights, & Resource Governance – Emerging Implications for USG Policies and Programming, USAID Property Rights and Resource Governance Project*. U.S. Agency for International Development, Washington DC.

Fukuyama, F., 2014. *Political Order and Political Decay: From the Industrial Revolution to the Globalization of Democracy*. Macmillan, New York, NY.

Geels, F. W., 2014. Regime resistance against low-carbon transitions: Introducing politics and power into the multi-level perspective. *Theory, Culture & Society* 31, 21–40. https://doi.org/10.1177/0263276414531627

Ghadge, A., Wurtmann, H., Seuring, S., 2020. Managing climate change risks in global supply chains: A review and research agenda. *International Journal of Production Research* 58, 44–64. https://doi.org/10.1080/00207543.2019.1629670

Gleick, P. H., 2014. Water, drought, climate change, and conflict in Syria. *Weather, Climate, and Society* 6, 331–340. https://doi.org/10.1175/WCAS-D-13-00059.1

Goodin, R. E. (Ed.), 1998. *The Theory of Institutional Design (Theories of Institutional Design)*. Cambridge University Press, Cambridge.

Gupta, J., Termeer, C., Klostermann, J., Meijerink, S., van den Brink, M., Jong, P., Nooteboom, S., Bergsma, E., 2010. The adaptive capacity wheel: A method to assess the inherent characteristics of institutions to enable the adaptive capacity of society. *Environmental Science & Policy* 13, 459–471. https://doi.org/10.1016/j.envsci.2010.05.006

Hale, T., 2018. Catalytic cooperation (No. BSG-WP-2018/026, September 2018), BSG Working Paper Series. Blavatnik School of Government, University of Oxford, Oxford, UK. www.bsg.ox.ac.uk/sites/default/files/2018-09/BSG-WP-2018-026.pdf

Hale, T., 2016. "All hands on deck": The Paris agreement and nonstate climate action. *Global Environmental Politics* 16, 12–22. https://doi.org/10.1162/GLEP_a_00362

Hale, T., Held, D., 2018. Breaking the cycle of gridlock. *Global Policy* 9, 129–137. https://doi.org/10.1111/1758–5899.12524

Hale, T., Held, D., Young, K., 2013. *Gridlock: Why Global Cooperation Is Failing When We Need It Most*. Polity Press, Cambridge, UK.

Hall, P. A., 2010. Chapter 7: Historical institutionalism in rationalist and sociological perspective, in: Mahoney, J., Thelen, K. (Eds.), *Explaining Institutional Change: Ambiguity, Agency, and Power.*. Cambridge University Press, Cambridge, 204–223.

Hall, P. A., 1993. Policy paradigms, social learning, and the state: The case of economic policymaking in Britain. *Comparative Politics* 25, 275. https://doi.org/10.2307/422246

Hall, P. A., Taylor, R. C. R., 1996. Political science and the three new institutionalisms. *Political Studies* 44, 936–957. https://doi.org/10.1111/j.1467–9248.1996.tb00343.x

Hausknost, D., Hammond, M., 2020. Beyond the environmental state? The political prospects of a sustainability transformation. *Environmental Politics* 29, 1–16. https://doi.org/10.1080/09644016.2020.1686204

Hayek, F. A., 1991. *The Road to Serfdom*. Routledge, London, UK.

Hodgson, G. M., 2006. What are institutions? *Journal of Economic Issues* 40, 1–25. https://doi.org/10.1080/00213624.2006.11506879

Hoffmann, M., 2011. *Climate Governance at the Crossroads Experimenting with a Global Response after Kyoto*. Oxford University Press, New York, NY.

Hommel, D., Murphy, A. B., 2013. Rethinking geopolitics in an era of climate change. *GeoJournal* 78, 507–524. https://doi.org/10.1007/s10708-012–9448-8

Hughes, S., 2017. The politics of urban climate change policy: Toward a research agenda. *Urban Affairs Review* 53, 362–380. https://doi.org/10.1177/1078087416649756

IPCC, 2018. (Intergovernmental Panel on Climate Change) Special Report on Global Warming of 1.5°C. Incheon, South Korea. www.ipcc.ch/sr15/download/

Jacobs, A. M., 2016. Policy making for the long term in advanced democracies. *Annual Review of Political Science* 19, 433–454. https://doi.org/10.1146/annurev-polisci-110813-034103

Jacobs, A. M., Weaver, R. K., 2015. When policies undo themselves: Self-undermining feedback as a source of policy change: Self-Undermining Feedback. *Governance* 28, 441–457. https://doi.org/10.1111/gove.12101

Johnstone, P., Newell, P., 2018. Sustainability transitions and the state. *Environmental Innovation and Societal Transitions* 27, 72–82. https://doi.org/10.1016/j.eist.2017.10.006

Jordan, A., Bauer, M. W., Green-Pedersen, C., 2013. Policy dismantling. *Journal of European Public Policy* 20, 795–805. https://doi.org/10.1080/13501763.2013.771092

Jordan, A., Huitema, D., 2014. Innovations in climate policy: The politics of invention, diffusion, and evaluation. *Environmental Politics* 23, 715–734. https://doi.org/10.1080/09644016.2014.923614

Jordan, A., Lenschow, A., 2010. Environmental policy integration: A state of the art review. *Environmental Policy and Governance* 20, 147–158. https://doi.org/10.1002/eet.539

Jordan, A., Matt, E., 2014. Designing policies that intentionally stick: Policy feedback in a changing climate. *Policy Sciences* 47, 227–247. https://doi.org/10.1007/s11077-014-9201-x

Jordan, A. J., Huitema, D., van Asselt, H., Forster, J., 2018. *Governing Climate Change: Polycentricity in Action?* Cambridge University Press, Cambridge, MA.

Kallis, G., Norgaard, R. B., 2010. Coevolutionary ecological economics. *Ecological Economics* 69, 690–699. https://doi.org/10.1016/j.ecolecon.2009.09.017

Kates, R. W., Travis, W. R., Wilbanks, T. J., 2012. Transformational adaptation when incremental adaptations to climate change are insufficient. *Proceedings of the National Academy of Sciences* 109, 7156–7161. https://doi.org/10.1073/pnas.1115521109

Kingston, C., Caballero, G., 2009. Comparing theories of institutional change. *Journal of Institutional Economics* 5, 151–180. https://doi.org/10.1017/S1744137409001283

Koelble, T. A., Siddle, A., 2014. Institutional complexity and unanticipated consequences: The failure of decentralization in South Africa. *Democratization* 21, 1117–1133. https://doi.org/10.1080/13510347 .2013.784270

Lawrence, T. B., Suddaby, R., Leca, B., 2009. *Institutional Work: Actors and Agency in Institutional Studies of Organizations*. Cambridge University Press, Cambridge.

Lieberman, R. C., 2002. Ideas, institutions, and political order: Explaining political change. *American Political Science Review* 96, 697–712.

Lockwood, M., Kuzemko, C., Mitchell, C., Hoggett, R., 2017. Historical institutionalism and the politics of sustainable energy transitions: A research agenda. *Environment and Planning C: Politics and Space* 35, 312–333. https://doi.org/10.1177/0263774X16660561

Loorbach, D., 2010. Transition management for sustainable development: A prescriptive, complexity-based governance framework. *Governance: An International Journal of Policy, Administration, and Institutions* 23, 161–183.

Loorbach, D., Frantzeskaki, N., Avelino, F., 2017. Sustainability transitions research: Transforming science and practice for societal change. *Annual Review of Environment and Resources* 42(1), 599–626. https://doi.org/ 10.1146/annurev-environ-102014-021340

Lorenzoni, I., Benson, D., 2014. Radical institutional change in environmental governance: Explaining the origins of the UK Climate Change Act 2008 through discursive and streams perspectives. *Global Environmental Change* 29, 10–21. https://doi.org/10.1016/j.gloenvcha.2014.07.011

Mahoney, J., Thelen, K. (Eds.), 2015. *Advances in Comparative-Historical Analysis*. Cambridge University Press, Cambridge.

Mahoney, J., Thelen, K., 2010. *Explaining Institutional Change: Ambiguity, Agency, and Power*. Cambridge University Press, New York, NY.

Maltzman, F., Shipan, C. R., 2008. Change, Continuity, and the Evolution of the Law. *American Journal of Political Science* 52, 252–267. https://doi.org/ 10.1111/j.1540–5907.2008.00311.x

March, J. G., Olsen, J. P., 2008. Elaborating the "new institutionalism," in: Rhodes, R. A. W., Binder, S. A., Rockman, B. A. (Eds.), *The Oxford Handbook of Political Institutions*. Oxford University Press, Oxford, UK, pp. 3–20.

March, J. G., Olsen, J. P., 1983. The new institutionalism: Organizational factors in political life. *American Political Science Review* 78, 734–749. https://doi.org/10.2307/1961840

McGuire, C. J., 2019. Chapter 7: An exploration of coastal property rights in the United States under conditions of sea level rise, in: Zavattaro, S. M., Peterson,

G. R., Davis, A. E. (Eds.), *Property Rights in Contemporary Governance*. State University of New York Press, Albany, NY, 109–125.

Meijer, A., van der Veer, R., Faber, A., Penning de Vries, J., 2017. Political innovation as ideal and strategy: The case of aleatoric democracy in the City of Utrecht. *Public Management Review* 19, 20–36. https://doi.org/10.1080/14719037.2016.1200666

Meijerink, S., Huitema, D., 2010. Policy entrepreneurs and change strategies: Lessons from sixteen case studies of water transitions around the globe. *Ecology and Society* 15, 21.

Milly, P. C. D., Betancourt, J., Falkenmark, M., Hirsch, R. M., Kundzewicz, Z. W., Lettenmaier, D. P., Stouffer, R. J., 2008. Stationarity is dead: Whither water management?*Science* 319, 573–574. https://doi.org/10.1126/science.1151915

Mitchell, R. B., 2006. Problem structure, institutional design, and the relative effectiveness of international environmental agreements. *Global Environmental Politics* 6, 72–89. https://doi.org/10.1162/glep.2006.6.3.72

Monstadt, J., Wolff, A., 2015. Energy transition or incremental change? Green policy agendas and the adaptability of the urban energy regime in Los Angeles. *Energy Policy* 78, 213–224. https://doi.org/10.1016/j.enpol.2014.10.022

Moore, M., Hartley, J., 2008. Innovations in governance. *Public Management Review* 10, 3–20. https://doi.org/10.1080/14719030701763161

Moser, S. C., Ekstrom, J. A., 2010. A framework to diagnose barriers to climate change adaptation. *Proceedings of the National Academy of Sciences* 107, 22026–22031. https://doi.org/10.1073/pnas.1007887107

Mossberger, K., Stoker, G., 2001. The evolution of urban regime theory: The challenge of conceptualization. *Urban Affairs Review* 36, 810–835. https://doi.org/10.1177/10780870122185109

Nardulli, P. F., Peyton, B., Bajjalieh, J., 2015. Climate change and civil unrest: The impact of rapid-onset disasters. *Journal of Conflict Resolution* 59, 310–335. https://doi.org/10.1177/0022002713503809

NCE, 2018. *Unlocking the inclusive growth story of the 21st century: Accelerating climate action in urgent times*. The New Climate Economy (NCE), The Global Commission on the Economy and Climate, World Resources Institute, Washington DC, and Overseas Development Institute, London, UK.

Newell, P., 2015. Chapter 5. The politics of green transformations in capitalism Peter Newell, in: Scoones, I., Leach, M., Newell, P. (Eds.), *The Politics of Green Transformations* (1st ed.).. Routledge, London; New York, NY, pp. 68–85.

Newell, P., Paterson, M., 2010. *Climate Capitalism: Global Warming and the Transformation of the Global Economy.* Cambridge University Press, Cambridge; New York, NY.

Newig, J., Derwort, P., Jager, N. W., 2019. Sustainability through institutional failure and decline? Archetypes of productive pathways. E&S 24, art18. https://doi.org/10.5751/ES-10700–240118

Norris, P., Inglehart, R., 2019. *Cultural Backlash: Trump, Brexit, and Authoritarian Populism*, 1st ed., Cambridge University Press, Cambridge, United Kingdom. https://doi.org/10.1017/9781108595841

North, D. C., 2010. Understanding the process of economic change, 10. print., and 1. paperback print. ed., *The Princeton Economic History of the Western World*. Princeton University Press, Princeton, NJ.

Oberthür, S., 2016. Regime-interplay management: Lessons from environmental policy and law, in: Blome, K., Fischer-Lescano, A., Franzki, H., Markard, N., Oeter, S. (Eds.), *Contested Regime Collisions*. Cambridge University Press, Cambridge, pp. 88–108. https://doi.org/10.1017/CBO9781316411230.005

Oberthür, S., Gehring, T., 2006a. Institutional interaction in global environmental governance: The case of the Cartagena Protocol and the World Trade Organization. *Global Environmental Politics* 6, 1–31.

Oberthür, S., Gehring, T. (Eds.), 2006b. *Institutional Interaction in Global Environmental Governance: Synergy and Conflict among International and EU Policies, Global Environmental Accord.* MIT Press, Cambridge, Massachusetts.

Oberthür, S., Stokke, O. S. (Eds.), 2011. *Managing Institutional Complexity: Regime Interplay and Global Environmental Change, Institutional Dimensions of Global Environmental Change.* MIT Press, Cambridge, Massachusetts.

Ocasio-Cortez, A., 2019. House Resolution 109 – 116th Congress (2019–2020): Green New Deal Resolution – Recognizing the duty of the Federal Government to create a Green New Deal. www.congress.gov/bill/116th-congress/house-resolution/109

Orren, K., Skowronek, S., 1996. Institutions and intercurrence: Theory building in the fullness of time. *Nomos* 38, 111–146.

Ostrom, E., 2005. *Understanding Institutional Diversity.* Princeton University Press, New Jersey, USA.

Ostrom, E., 1990. *Governing the Commons: The Evolution of Institutions for Collective Action.* Cambridge University Press, Cambridge, United Kingdom.

Ostrom, V., Tiebout, C. M., Warren, R., 1961. The organization of government in metropolitan areas: A theoretical inquiry. *The American Political Science Review* 55, 831. https://doi.org/10.2307/1952530

Otto, I. M., Donges, J. F., Cremades, R., Bhowmik, A., Hewitt, R. J., Lucht, W., Rockström, J., Allerberger, F., McCaffrey, M., Doe, S. S. P., Lenferna, A., Morán, N., van Vuuren, D. P., Schellnhuber, H. J., 2020. Social tipping dynamics for stabilizing Earth's climate by 2050. *Proceedings of the National Academy of Sciences of the United States of America* 117, 2354–2365. https://doi.org/10.1073/pnas.1900577117

Partzsch, L., 2017. "Power with" and "power to" in environmental politics and the transition to sustainability. *Environmental Politics* 26, 193–211. https://doi.org/10.1080/09644016.2016.1256961

Patashnik, E. M., 2014. *Reforms at Risk: What Happens after Major Policy Changes Are Enacted*. Princeton University Press, Princeton.

Patterson, J., Schulz, K., Vervoort, J., van der Hel, S., Widerberg, O., Adler, C., Hurlbert, M., Anderton, K., Sethi, M., Barau, A., 2017. Exploring the governance and politics of transformations towards sustainability. *Environmental Innovation and Societal Transitions* 24, 1–16. https://doi.org/10.1016/j.eist.2016.09.001

Patterson, J., Voogt, D. L., Sapiains, R., 2019. Beyond inputs and outputs: Process-oriented explanation of institutional change in climate adaptation governance. *Environmental Policy and Governance* 29, 360–375. https://doi.org/10.1002/eet.1865

Patterson, J. J., 2019. *Chapter 8: Agency and Architecture: Producing Stability and Change, in: Agency in Earth System Governance* (Eds. Betsill, M., Gerlak, A. K., Benney, T. M.). Cambridge University Press.

Patterson, J. J., Beunen, R., 2019. Institutional work in environmental governance. *Journal of Environmental Planning and Management* 62(3), 1–11. https://doi.org/10.1080/09640568.2018.1538328

Patterson, J. J., Huitema, D., 2019. Institutional innovation for adapting to climate change in urban governance. *Journal of Environmental Planning and Management* 62(3), 374–398. https://doi.org/10.1080/09640568.2018.1510767

Patterson, J. J., Thaler, T., Hoffmann, M., Hughes, S., Oels, A., Chu, E., Mert, A., Huitema, D., Burch, S., Jordan, A., 2018. Political feasibility of 1.5°C societal transformations: The role of social justice. *Current Opinion in Environmental Sustainability* 31, 1–9. https://doi.org/10.1016/j.cosust.2017.11.002

Peel, J., Osofsky, H. M., 2018. A rights turn in climate change litigation? *Transnational Environmental Law* 7, 37–67. https://doi.org/10.1017/S2047102517000292

Pelling, M., 2011. *Adaptation to Climate Change: From Resilience to Transformation*. Routledge, London & New York, NY.

Peng, Y., Bai, X., 2018. Experimenting towards a low-carbon city: Policy evolution and nested structure of innovation. *Journal of Cleaner Production* 174, 201–212. https://doi.org/10.1016/j.jclepro.2017.10.116

Peters, B. G., 2015. State failure, governance failure and policy failure: Exploring the linkages. *Public Policy and Administration* 30, 261–276. https://doi.org/10.1177/0952076715581540

Pierson, P., 2004. *Politics in Time: History, Institutions, and Social Analysis.* Princeton University Press, Princeton, New Jersey.

Pierson, P., 2000a. Increasing returns, path dependence, and the study of politics. *The American Political Science Review* 94, 251. https://doi.org/10.2307/2586011

Pierson, P., 2000b. The limits of design: Explaining institutional origins and change. *Governance* 13, 475–499. https://doi.org/10.1111/0952–1895.00142

Pierson, P., 1993. When effect becomes cause: Policy feedback and political change. *World Politics* 45, 595–628. https://doi.org/10.2307/2950710

Prakash, A., Potoski, M., 2016. Dysfunctional institutions? Toward a new agenda in governance studies: Institutional & governance gailure. *Regulation & Governance* 10, 115–125. https://doi.org/10.1111/rego.12113

Pralle, S. B., 2009. Agenda-setting and climate change. *Environmental Politics* 18, 781–799. https://doi.org/10.1080/09644010903157115

Raworth, K., 2017. *Doughnut Economics: Seven Ways to Think Like a 21st-Century Economist.* Chelsea Green Publishing, UK.

Rhodes, R. A. W., Binder, S. A., Rockman, B. A. (Eds.), 2008. *The Oxford Handbook of Political Institutions.* Oxford University Press, Oxford. DOI: 10.1093/oxfordhb/9780199548460.001.0001

Rittel, H. W. J., Webber, M. M., 1973. Dilemmas in a general theory of planning. *Policy Sciences* 4, 155–169.

Roberts, C., Geels, F. W., 2019. Conditions for politically accelerated transitions: Historical institutionalism, the multi-level perspective, and two historical case studies in transport and agriculture. *Technological Forecasting and Social Change* 140, 221–240. https://doi.org/10.1016/j.techfore.2018.11.019

Roberts, C., Geels, F. W., Lockwood, M., Newell, P., Schmitz, H., Turnheim, B., Jordan, A., 2018. The politics of accelerating low-carbon transitions: Towards a new research agenda. *Energy Research & Social Science* 44, 304–311. https://doi.org/10.1016/j.erss.2018.06.001

Rosenbloom, D., 2017. Pathways: An emerging concept for the theory and governance of low-carbon transitions. *Global Environmental Change* 43, 37–50. https://doi.org/10.1016/j.gloenvcha.2016.12.011

Sabatier, P. A. (Ed.), 2007. *Theories of the Policy Process*, 2nd ed., Westview Press, Boulder, Colo.

Sachs, N. M., 2012. Can we regulate our way to energy efficiency: Product standards as climate policy. *Vanderbilt Law Review* 65, 1631–1678.

Schaller, S., Carius, A., 2019. *Convenient Truths: Mapping Climate Agendas of Right-Wing Populist Parties in Europe.* Adelphi Consult GmbH, Berlin.

Schmidt, V. A., 2008. Discursive institutionalism: The explanatory power of ideas and discourse. *Annual Review of Political Science* 11, 303–326. https://doi.org/10.1146/annurev.polisci.11.060606.135342

Schot, J., Geels, F. W., 2008. Strategic niche management and sustainable innovation journeys: Theory, findings, research agenda, and policy. *Technology Analysis & Strategic Management* 20, 537–554. https://doi.org/10.1080/09537320802292651

Scoones, I., Leach, M., Newell, P. (Eds.), 2015. *The Politics of Green Transformations, Pathways to Sustainability.* Routledge, London; New York, NY.

Sellers, S., Ebi, K. L., Hess, J., 2019. Climate change, human health, and social stability: Addressing interlinkages. *Environmental Health Perspectives* 127, 045002. https://doi.org/10.1289/EHP4534

Sen, A., 2009. *The Idea of Justice.* The Belknap Press of Harvard University Press, Cambridge, MA, United States.

Seto, K. C., Davis, S. J., Mitchell, R. B., Stokes, E. C., Unruh, G., Ürge-Vorsatz, D., 2016. Carbon lock-in: Types, causes, and policy implications. *Annual Review of Environment and Resources* 41, 425–452.

Sharp, B. T., 2019. Stepping into the breach: State constitutions as vehicle for advancing rights-based climate litigation. *Duke Journal of Constitutional Law and Public Policy Sidebar* 14, 39–74.

Sheingate, A., 2014. Institutional dynamics and American political development. *Annual Review of Political Science* 17, 461–477. https://doi.org/10.1146/annurev-polisci-040113-161139

Shi, L., Varuzzo, A. M., 2020. Surging seas, rising fiscal stress: Exploring municipal fiscal vulnerability to climate change. *Cities* 100, 102658. https://doi.org/10.1016/j.cities.2020.102658

Shipan, C. R., Volden, C., 2012. Policy diffusion: Seven lessons for scholars and practitioners. *Public Administration Review* 72, 788–796. https://doi.org/10.1111/j.1540–6210.2012.02610.x

Skovgaard, J., van Asselt, H., 2019. The politics of fossil fuel subsidies and their reform: Implications for climate change mitigation. *WIREs Climate Change* 10, e581. https://doi.org/10.1002/wcc.581

Sørensen, E., 2017. Political innovations: Innovations in political institutions, processes and outputs. *Public Management Review* 19, 1–19. https://doi.org/10.1080/14719037.2016.1200661

Stokes, L. C., 2016. Electoral backlash against climate policy: A natural experiment on retrospective voting and local resistance to public policy. *American Journal of Political Science* 60, 958–974. https://doi.org/10.1111/ajps.12220

Stoker, G., Mossberger, K., 1994. Urban regime theory in comparative perspective. *Environ Plann C Gov Policy* 12, 195–212. https://doi.org/10.1068/c120195

Stone, C., 1989. *Regime Politics*. University Press of Kansas, Lawrence, Kansas, United States.

Strang, D., Soule, S. A., 1998. Diffusion in organizations and social movements: From hybrid corn to poison pills. *Annual Review of Sociology* 24, 265–290. https://doi.org/10.1146/annurev.soc.24.1.265

Streeck, W., Thelen, K. A. (Eds.), 2005. *Beyond Continuity: Institutional Change in Advanced Political Economies*. Oxford University Press, Oxford; New York, NY.

Stripple, J., Bulkeley, H., 2019. Towards a material politics of socio-technical transitions: Navigating decarbonisation pathways in Malmö. *Political Geography* 72, 52–63. https://doi.org/10.1016/j.polgeo.2019.04.001

Thelen, K., 1999. Historical institutionalism in comparative politics. *Annual Review of Political Science* 2, 369–404. https://doi.org/10.1146/annurev.polisci.2.1.369

Torrens, J., Schot, J., Raven, R., Johnstone, P., 2019. Seedbeds, harbours, and battlegrounds: On the origins of favourable environments for urban experimentation with sustainability. *Environmental Innovation and Societal Transitions* 31, 211–232. https://doi.org/10.1016/j.eist.2018.11.003

Tosun, J., Lang, A., 2017. Policy integration: Mapping the different concepts. *Policy Studies* 38, 553–570. https://doi.org/10.1080/01442872.2017.1339239

Tsebelis, G., 2002. *Veto Players: How Political Institutions Work*. Princeton University Press, Princeton, New Jersey.

Turnheim, B., Asquith, M., Geels, F. W., 2020. Making sustainability transitions research policy-relevant: Challenges at the science-policy interface. *Environmental Innovation and Societal Transitions* 34, 116–120. https://doi.org/10.1016/j.eist.2019.12.009

Turnheim, B., Berkhout, F., Geels, F., Hof, A., McMeekin, A., Nykvist, B., van Vuuren, D., 2015. Evaluating sustainability transitions pathways: Bridging analytical approaches to address governance challenges. *Global Environmental Change* 35, 239–253. https://doi.org/10.1016/j.gloenvcha.2015.08.010

Turnheim, B., Geels, F. W., 2012. Regime destabilisation as the flipside of energy transitions: Lessons from the history of the British coal industry (1913–1997). *Energy Policy* 50, 35–49. https://doi.org/10.1016/j.enpol.2012.04.060

Unruh, G. C., 2002. Escaping carbon lock-in. *Energy Policy* 30, 317–325. https://doi.org/10.1016/S0301-4215(01)00098-2

Unruh, G. C., 2000. Understanding carbon lock-in. *Energy Policy* 28, 817–830. https://doi.org/10.1016/S0301-4215(00)00070-7

van Asselt, H., 2014. *The Fragmentation of Global Climate Governance: Consequences and Management of Regime Interactions (New Horizons in Environmental and Energy Law).* Edward Elgar, Cheltenham, UK; Northampton, MA, USA.

van den Bergh, J. C. J. M., 2007. Evolutionary thinking in environmental economics. *Journal of Evolutionary Economics* 17, 521–549. https://doi.org/10.1007/s00191-006-0054-0

van den Bergh, J. C. J. M., Truffer, B., Kallis, G., 2011. Environmental innovation and societal transitions: Introduction and overview. *Environmental Innovation and Societal Transitions* 1, 1–23. https://doi.org/10.1016/j.eist.2011.04.010

Victor, D. G., 2011. *Global Warming Gridlock: Creating More Effective Strategies for Protecting the Planet.* Cambridge University Press, Cambridge. https://doi.org/10.1017/CBO9780511975714

Wagenaar, H., Wood, M., 2018. The precarious politics of public innovation. *Politics and Governance* 6, 150. https://doi.org/10.17645/pag.v6i1.1275

Wenta, J., McDonald, J., McGee, J. S., March 2019. Enhancing resilience and justice in climate adaptation laws. *Transnational Environmental Law* 8(1), 89–118. https://doi.org/10.1017/S2047102518000286

Werz, M., Hoffman, M., 2016. Europe's twenty-first century challenge: Climate change, migration and security. *European View* 15, 145–154. https://doi.org/10.1007/s12290-016-0385-7

Westley, F., Olsson, P., Folke, C., Homer-dixon, T., Vredenburg, H., Loorbach, D., Thompson, J., Nilsson, M., Lambin, E., Sendzimir, J., Banerjee, B., Galaz, V., van der Leeuw, S., 2011. Tipping toward sustainability: Emerging pathways of transformation. *Ambio* 40, 762–780.

Weyland, K., 2008. Toward a new theory of institutional change. *World Politics* 60, 281–314. https://doi.org/10.1353/wp.0.0013

Whitmee, S., Haines, A., Beyrer, C., Boltz, F., Capon, A. G., de Souza Dias, B. F., Ezeh, A., Frumkin, H., Gong, P., Head, P., Horton, R., Mace, G. M., Marten, R., Myers, S. S., Nishtar, S., Osofsky, S. A., Pattanayak, S. K., Pongsiri, M. J., Romanelli, C., Soucat, A., Vega, J., Yach, D., 2015. Safeguarding human health in the Anthropocene epoch: Report of The Rockefeller Foundation–Lancet Commission on planetary health. *The Lancet* 386, 1973–2028. https://doi.org/10.1016/S0140-6736(15)60901-1

Wise, R. M., Fazey, I., Stafford Smith, M., Park, S. E., Eakin, H. C., Archer Van Garderen, E. R. M., Campbell, B., 2014. Reconceptualising adaptation to climate change as part of pathways of change and response. *Global Environmental Change* 28, 325–336. https://doi.org/10.1016/j.gloenvcha.20 13.12.002

Wright, E. O., 2010. *Envisioning Real Utopias*. Verso, London; New York, NY.

Young, O. R., 2013. Sugaring off: Enduring insights from long-term research on environmental governance. *International Environmental Agreements* 13, 87–105. https://doi.org/10.1007/s10784-012-9204-z

Young, O. R., 2010a. *Institutional Dynamics: Emergent Patterns in International Environmental Governance, Earth System Governance: A Core Research Project of the International Human Dimensions Programme on Global Environmental Change*. MIT Press, Cambridge, Massachusetts.

Young, O. R., 2010b. Institutional dynamics: Resilience, vulnerability and adaptation in environmental and resource regimes. *Global Environmental Change* 20, 378–385. https://doi.org/10.1016/j.gloenvcha.2009.10.001

Young, O. R., 2002. Chapter 8. Institutional Interplay: The Environmental Consequences of Cross-Scale Interactions, In: "The Drama of the Commons," Ostrom, E., Dietz, T., Dolsak, N., Stern, P. C., Stonich, S., Weber, E. U. (Eds.), in: *Committee on the Human Dimensions of Global Change. Division of Behavioral and Social Sciences and Education National Research Council*, National Academy Press, Washington, DC., pp. 263–292.

Young, O. R., King, L. A., Schroeder, H. (Eds.), 2008. *Institutions and Environmental Change: Principal Findings, Applications, and Research Frontiers*. MIT Press, Cambridge, Massachusetts.

Zelli, F., van Asselt, H., 2013. Introduction: The institutional fragmentation of global environmental governance: Causes, consequences, and responses. *Global Environmental Politics* 13, 1–13. https://doi.org/10.1162/GLEP_a_00180

Cambridge Elements ≡

Elements of Earth System Governance

Frank Biermann

Utrecht University

Frank Biermann is Research Professor of Global Sustainability Governance with the Copernicus Institute of Sustainable Development, Utrecht University, the Netherlands. He is the founding Chair of the Earth System Governance Project, a global transdisciplinary research network launched in 2009, and editor-in-chief of the new peer-reviewed journal *Earth System Governance* (Elsevier). In April 2018, he won a European Research Council Advanced Grant for a research program on the steering effects of the sustainable development goals.

Aarti Gupta

Wageningen University

Aarti Gupta is Professor of Global Environmental Governance at the Environmental Policy Group of Wageningen University, the Netherlands. She has been a lead faculty in the Earth System Governance Project since 2014 and served as one of five coordinating lead authors of the recently issued New Directions ESG Science and Implementation Plan. As of November 2018, she is a member of the ESG Project's Scientific Steering Committee. She is also associate editor of the journal *Global Environmental Politics*.

About the series

Linked with the Earth System Governance Project, this exciting new series will provide concise but authoritative studies of the governance of complex socio-ecological systems, written by world-leading scholars. Highly interdisciplinary in scope, the series will address governance processes and institutions at all levels of decision-making, from local to global, within a planetary perspective that seeks to align current institutions and governance systems with the fundamental twenty-first-century challenges of global environmental change and earth system transformations.

Elements in this series will present cutting-edge scientific research, while also seeking to contribute innovative transformative ideas toward better governance. A key aim of the series is to present policy-relevant research that is of interest to both academics and policymakers working on earth system governance.

More information about the Earth System Governance project can be found at: www.earthsystemgovernance.org

Cambridge Elements ☰

Elements of Earth System Governance

Elements in the series

Deliberative Global Governance
John S. Dryzek et al.

Environmental Rights in Earth System Governance: Democracy Beyond Democracy
Walter F. Baber and Robert V. Bartlett

The Making of Responsible Innovation
Phil Macnaghten

Environmental Recourse at the Multilateral Development Banks
Susan Park

A full series listing is available at www.cambridge.org/EESG

Printed in the United States
By Bookmasters